ACCLAIM

"Ed and Deb Shapiro are two warm, caring and capable individuals. Their work makes our planet a safer and more loving place to live."

—Dr. Bernie Siegel M.D., bestselling author
Love, Medicine and Miracles

"I can be as nuts as the next person, living in a world like we live in with the craziness and chaos. It takes work to retain our sanity in the midst of all that, and to me meditation is the most powerful tool for doing so."

—Marianne Williamson, New York Times bestselling author *A Return to Love*

"I hope that your work is reaching many. It deserves it and so do they."

—International bestselling author, Stephen Levine

"Ed and Deb bring compassion and heart to a modern world where it is sorely needed."

—Ram Dass, author of *Be Here Now and Still Here*

"If there is one book you read about Meditation this should be the one. Hear about some of the cool people who do it, why you should do it, and how."

—Sharon Gannon, Jivamukti Yoga

"What an accomplishment! Ed and Deb's profoundly unique book offers a one-stop-shop for those engaged in mindfulness and meditation. The direct transmission contained in this book can take us one step further. We find it especially useful to help stabilize spiritual activism in these challenging times and we'll refer it widely."
—Transpartisan activists John Steiner and Margo King

"Acceptance of what is, that is meditation. This book will help you make friends with your mind. Ed and Deb are spreading love in the world; be a part of it!"
—Parmita Pushman, White Swan Records

"The pausing has been profound. It has invited me to arrive in the here and now with my child clients, and to accept whatever happens without judging."
—Play therapist Megan Cronin Larson

"Mindfulness is the awareness that arises when we pay attention to the present moment. It accesses us to core aspects of our mind that our very sanity depends on, as does our capacity to live wholeheartedly in this crazy world."
—Mindfulness teacher Jon Kabat-Zinn

"The wonderful Shapiros are a conduit of joy and spiritual energy that heals hearts on their subtle level."
—Dr. Lex Hixon

"Ed and Deb make a connection to their friends spirit. They then bring their spiritual energy all over the world for world peace."
—Golden globe Award recipient and Grammy Award winning musician, Kitaro

"I know Ed and Deb as their television producer and they walk their talk."
—Joanne Sawicki, creator of Channel Health TV

The Unexpected Power Of Mindfulness & Meditation

Ed and Deb Shapiro

To Deb's mother, Anne, and to our
teachers, both past and present.
May all beings be happy.

Acknowledgments

Our deep thanks to Bill Gladstone, for his inspiration and support. To Abby Bergman for her joyful tirelessness. To David Nelson, Jim & Jane & Splash Cronin, Rob & Megan Cronin Larson & Dakota, Kiri Westby, Helen Green, Julie Carpenter, Mache & Sharon Siebel, and Raji & Rani. And a big thank you to all the contributors, you make this book glow with wisdom.

Contents

Part Two
How To Do It

Part Three
The Fruits of Silence

Foreword

Thank goodness Ed and Deb have so beautifully enfolded the gifts of the fascinating individuals in this book, within the moving stories of their own transforming experiences! In this living book they have masterfully woven the many voices into a symphony—the insights harmonize and contrast with each other in a marvelous rich flow that is both calming and energizing, creating a single collective yet selfless voice.

Reading this book is itself a powerful meditation. Without even trying, you effortlessly go deeper into your mind and heart. By flowing along page-by-page, teacher-by-teacher, insight-by-insight you will find you are naturally developing mindfulness.

What a privilege to strike a key chord at the opening of this treasury of heartfelt advice by many of the greatest people you would ever hope to meet, all seasoned and realized meditators, way beyond me! And what a challenge to partner with Ed and Deb to move this magical meditation train along toward the meaningful life that is the destination for every single one of you dear readers!

I only dare proceed because I find a job for myself here with this miracle train, where the engine is the great heart of all spiritual teachers, visionaries and poets throughout the world from all times; the kind and skillful engineers are Ed and Deb; and the cars you ride in so comfortably are the spacious realizations of all the great meditators who carry you along.

I am just the conductor who sees you up the steps, shouts out "Aaaallll abooooaaaard!" and then swings up alongside you all! Congratulations for embarking on this very special and magical journey.

Tenzin Bob Thurman
Jey Tsong Kappa Professor of Indo-Tibetan Buddhist Studies,
Columbia University
President, Tibet House, US

Part One
All You Need To Know

1 ABCs

Starting off my day without meditation would be like going to work without brushing my teeth. Russell Simmons

Transforming Ourselves

It's happening! Mindfulness and meditation are merging into our lives like good friends. On the wall behind the counter in our local post office, fliers advertising meditation and yoga classes hang next to the overseas postal prices; cross-legged yogis and Buddhist monks are seen in advertisements for everything from computers to cars; major magazines and websites carry stories on the benefits of mindfulness and meditation with tips from famous celebrities, such as Lady Gaga or Oprah, Sting or Madonna; and no self-respecting bookshop is without a how-to-meditate section.

It is no longer necessary to be a hippie or on a spiritual quest in order to meditate. We have taught everyone from housewives to athletes, musicians, therapists and CEOs, in yoga centers and town halls, high school gymnasiums, living rooms, corporate boardrooms, and on television.

However, this poses a conundrum. If mindfulness and meditation are so available and well known, and if health reports are saying we should all be practicing them, why do so many people ignore them or find excuses not to try? How ironic that the best things for us are those we avoid the most, which is like being addicted to poison while resisting the antidote.

We both discovered the wonder of meditation early on in our lives—Ed was a part of the 'love generation' and living in a commune in New York City, Deb was just fifteen and living in London—and we love to share this greatest thing mankind has ever discovered: the art of being still. Also, it's a very cool thing to do.

> "Meditation, past calming our nerves, past being good for our blood pressure, past working out our own internal psychological dramas, which it does, past helping us to get along with our kin and our community, is a way of seeing the truth that the only way to ameliorate our suffering is to keep our minds clear," says meditation teacher **Sylvia Boorstein.**

There is a sanity and brilliance to mindfulness and meditation, from awakening inner strength, kindness and fearlessness to inviting radical change to every aspect of our lives.

So the equation is simple: as meditation becomes an intimate part of our lives, so we evolve and change. When we evolve and change then we move into a more wakeful, wise, and loving state. And all that we have to do for this chain of events to occur is learn to be still.

The opposite of this is discomfort, stress, and suffering, usually due to the desire for things to be different from how they are and the longing to escape from what is seen as a dissatisfying present. The word suffering comes from the Pali word *dukkha,* which means not only suffering but includes all its varied family relations, such as discomfort, pain, anguish, dissatisfaction, failure, conflict, hurt. What do we do when one of these comes knocking at our door? How do we maintain our balance?

"We are typically rushing past our experiences; we rehearse what we want to say, recollect what we should have done, hoping, fearing, living in drama," says author **Michael Carroll**. "In meditation we can observe this internal drama, chatter and panic, and discover a profound depth to our lives that had previously been overlooked."

Meditation is that rare activity that eases suffering while developing the awareness to move beyond the unawareness that caused the suffering in the first place.

"Like a drama queen, I always felt my emotions very intensely, so the typical egotistical stories that I told myself were: you're a fraud, you open your mouth and nothing will come out, everyone else is here at Harvard because of merit but you're here because of some bizarre error, you don't belong here, soon they will find out unless you do everything perfectly," says inspirational teacher **Joan Borysenko**.

"One day, one of my lab partners said, 'You know, you actually believe what goes on in your mind, and you're always manufacturing really scary stories.' I was aghast; it was so true. Then he said, 'When I meditate I don't buy into the stories the same way anymore.' I tried it and he was absolutely right. It totally changed my relationship to the story."

Chaos is natural—the universe is organized chaos—so to find inner peace in the midst of this is vital. Sanity comes by having an attitude of non-grasping. If we hold on, whether to resentment, irritation, hurt, or even anger, more suffering is generated. Our mind gets caught up in the emotion and we lose our balance. Letting go doesn't deny our feelings, but it keeps us connected to awareness.

"The effect of meditation can show up in real-life situations where maybe somebody is pushing our buttons and we would normally respond in an aggressive and habitual response," says yoga teacher **Cyndi Lee**.

"When we are mindful of our feelings, we can recognize what is arising in time to let it go. In that gap, we can make a choice of the action we want to take, instead of thoughtlessly reacting. Without that awareness, we have no options."

Think of the water in a lake. When the water is disturbed then we get caught up in the waves and turmoil, but when the water is calm then the still depths below can be seen clearly. Beneath the dramas and conflicts there is a very sane and calm place to rest in.

Meditation is an invitation to abide in that stillness. No longer restricted by a narrow worldview, we step into a bigger, more inclusive picture, greater than the story and our part in it.

The unexpected power of this book is that it not only explains what mindfulness and meditation are and how to practice them, but it also reveals that, at the same time, you will be transforming your life from the inside out. Which is the best part.

M and M: What's The Difference?

"In any one day there are moments where there is nothing going on, but we link up what is happening from thought to thought without any space. We overlook the spaciousness that it's all happening in," says spiritual teacher **Gangaji.**

Nowadays, mindfulness and meditation are often used to mean the same thing, which can be confusing, while not many are clear on what 'mindfulness meditation' is and how it differs from either of the above. So here's our version:

Mindfulness is being aware. It's noticing and paying attention to thoughts, feelings, behavior, and everything else. Mindfulness can be practiced at any time, wherever we are, whoever we are with, and whatever we are doing, by showing up and being fully engaged in the here and now.

That means being free of both the past and future—the what if's and what maybe's—and free of judgment of right or wrong—the I'm-the-best and I'm-no-good scenarios—so that we can be totally present without distraction.

"Mindfulness is the awareness that arises when we non-judgmentally pay attention in the present moment. It cultivates access to core aspects of our own minds and bodies that our very sanity depends on," says mindfulness teacher **Jon Kabat-Zinn.**

"Mindfulness, which includes tenderness and kindness toward ourselves, restores dimensions of our being. These have never actually been missing, just that we have been missing them, we have been absorbed elsewhere. When your mind clarifies and opens, your heart also clarifies and opens.

"And mindful awareness is not missing the light shimmering from the snow hanging off the roof outside the window and from the hemlock tree beyond it, because you are too preoccupied with your own thoughts. It's not being so self-centered that you fail to notice what is going on around you."

Mindfulness happens to also release 'happy' chemicals in the brain so we feel great; it lowers blood pressure, improves digestion, and relaxes tension around pain. It is simple to practice and wonderful in effect.

Not a bad deal when all that is needed is to pay attention, which sounds like something we should all be doing but often forget. When we do pay attention, then change becomes possible.

"Einstein said that we can't solve our problems from the level of thinking that we were at when we created them," says motivational speaker **Marianne Williamson**. "A different level of thinking doesn't mean just a different emphasis in our thinking, or a more loving kind of thinking. It means what he said, a different level of thinking, and, to me, that is what meditation is.

"Meditation changes us, as it returns us to our right mind."

Mindfulness and meditation are mirror-like reflections of each other: mindfulness supports and enriches meditation, while meditation nurtures and expands mindfulness. While mindfulness can be applied to any situation throughout the day, meditation is usually practiced for a specific amount of time.

"I don't make a difference between meditating and having my life," says meditation teacher **Sylvia Boorstein.** "I am mindful of the presence or absence of my capacity to care. In this moment, am I bringing attention to whatever I am doing? Is my mind generating good thoughts about other people? Formal periods of mediation simply point me in the direction of how I want to live during the whole day."

There are many forms of meditation. Some are aimed at developing a clear and focused mind, known as 'Clear Mind' meditations. Others are aimed at developing altruistic states, such as loving kindness, compassion or forgiveness, known as 'Open Heart' meditations. Others use the body as a means to develop awareness, such as yoga or walking; others use sound, as in chanting or intoning sacred words.

"I could never still my mind. And then, as I was approaching my seventieth birthday, I thought the time has come," says actress **Jane Fonda**. "Part of getting older is that as the externals begin to fray so you are beckoned inward. As my mind became quieter in meditation, I discovered this place that seemed to be suspended behind my forehead, like a chandelier hanging from the top of my skull. It was a place of complete stillness."

Mindfulness Meditation is a form of Clear Mind meditation. Attention is paid to the natural rhythm of the breath while sitting, and to the rhythm of slow walking. This alone can have an enormous impact.

Ultimately, meditation is spontaneous and natural, just as when we go to bed at night and sleep seems to come by itself. The method is simply an aide, just as a hammer can help build a house but is not the house.

Meditation practice is not an end in itself; it is the means, like a ferryboat that takes us across a river. We may wander off and do all sorts of other things, but the stillness of meditation will always be there, waiting. It is a companion to have throughout our life, like an old friend we turn to when in need of direction, inspiration, and clarity. There is no right or wrong way to practice, as we all do it differently. Most important of all, meditation is to be enjoyed!

Neither mindfulness nor meditation belong to any particular religion or philosophy, any thought programming, or to any political party. Every religion has its own form of meditation (as in prayer), as does every philosophy (as in self-reflection). For instance, Deb used to join her Quaker grandparents at Sunday meetings, where they would sit together in silence.

"The children came from their Sunday school to join the adult group for the last fifteen minutes," recalls **Deb**. "I used to squeeze in next to my grandfather, and instantly I was merging into the silence.

"One day my grandmother was moved to speak. She stood up and said quite emphatically, 'Even if it is a cloudy day, the sun is always shining!' Then she sat down. Being a child, I was highly embarrassed and longed to giggle, but the silence simply absorbed both her words and my laughter."

We were at Barnes & Noble in New York, holding a book signing with some of the authors quoted in this book. After the talk we asked if there were any questions. A lady at the back stood up and asked, "What's the difference between prayer and meditation?" The actress, Ellen Burstyn, chose to answer. She said, "Prayer is when you talk with God, and meditation is when you listen."

"The essence of prayer is praise and thank you," says theologian **Matthew Fox**. "The essence of meditation is being still, and out of the stillness there comes a great gratitude. It works the other way too, as prayer encourages stillness and silence. So prayer is like being on a raft on a rushing river, which is meditation in its deepest form."

Being Here Now

Someone once asked Ed if he had ever experienced another dimension. He replied, "Have you ever experienced this one?"

Sitting still can easily seem boring. The mind longs to be entertained! So instead of stillness, we fill our minds either with what-could-have-been, what-might-have-been or if-only, or with what-could-be, what-will-be or what-might-be. In fact, past or future can become so engrossing that being in the present moment may seem somewhat lackluster in comparison.

However, the development of present-moment awareness is immensely liberating. There is nothing going on but this very moment, nothing more is required of us than to just be here, now. What a relief!

When we are present then the world becomes extraordinary, as if being seen and heard for the first time without preconceived ideas or desires. There is just the experience. But like a child exploring the unknown, we are impelled to understand and know it more intimately.

Such awareness takes us out of the logical or rational mind, which doesn't mean we step into nowhere or nothingness; we don't become disconnected or cast adrift. Rather, we step into sanity and even greater connectedness. It is innately natural, as if we are remembering a loved but forgotten place.

"When I was 15 years old, my mother took me on a residential meditation retreat in the English country-side," recalls **Deb**. "My siblings were all elsewhere and my mother had no intention of leaving me in London on my own. As I already knew some of the people who would be there, and as she was only going for three days, I reluctantly agreed.

"As it was, my mother stayed for three days and I stayed for ten. I don't think I really understood what I was meant to be doing, but sitting in silence gave me the feeling that I was exactly where I was meant to be. I sat for hours. I didn't want to leave. I didn't want to be parted from this place of belonging. I was home again, even though I didn't know that I had ever left."

Simply being still, without thought of before or after, encourages a deep sense of completion, that there really is nowhere else we need to go. It is impossible to think of somewhere else as being better—the grass is vividly green exactly where we are.

For instance, we were in England visiting with Deb's mother, Anne. We had all been invited for tea at the House of Lord's in London to discuss a meditation center. In a rush to catch a train we were quickly downing breakfast when the toast burned. We watched in amusement as Anne took a deep breath and said, "Oh dear, burned toast," then calmly tossed the offending article in the trash and put a fresh slice of bread in the toaster.

Few of us have such a calm reaction to burned toast, especially when we're in a hurry. But Anne displayed the same attitude of calm acceptance later that day when we were having tea in London.

Now, being invited to the House of Lords does not happen every day. It is a stunningly beautiful old building, seeped in history and tradition. We sat in the chambers and listened to a debate; we walked through the Queen's robbing room where her throne sits; and then we went for tea and cakes.

The regal Tea Rooms sound quintessentially English and we fully expected the tea to be of good English quality. The room was spectacular, the silver service was everything we could have wanted, but the cakes were not—they were old and dry—not good Brit fare at all!

Simply being with what is showed itself as Anne delicately ate her unappetizing chocolate éclair without a single complaint. Usually we wish things were different to how they are, whether it's the big things like our partner or job, or the small things like the weather or chocolate éclairs. But we can make a song and dance about burned toast and get even more stressed, or we can take a deep breath and get a fresh slice of bread.

"If I accept burnt toast as a 'fact', somehow that takes away the irritation I normally feel and replaces it with a wry admiration for the splendidly black crusts," says author **Anne Bancroft**. "It doesn't stop me changing the setting of the toaster but it seems to make the whole situation easy instead of annoying."

More Happy

We were in Thailand, attending a ten-day silent meditation retreat in the middle of a coconut grove. Every day Ajahn Maha Dharma Tan, a Thai monk, would come to teach, and each day he would ask us the same question: "Are you happier today than you were yesterday?"

As he said this, a wide smile would fill his face because he knew that we were confronting numerous obstacles to happiness, and not just the ones in our own minds. As beautiful as the coconut grove was, we were living with mosquitoes, centipedes and snakes, sleeping on wooden pallets, and had no food after midday. How were we expected to find happiness amidst such extremes?

Yet despite his humorous tone, the monk's question was a genuine one. We were on a meditation retreat. If we weren't beginning to feel happier as a result, then we were missing the point of being there.

Every day for ten days, he asked us: "Are you happier today than you were yesterday?"

This simple question exposed how easily negative habits and self-obsession could dominate our way of thinking. It showed us how hard it was to trust happiness, even that we could forget what happiness meant. How easy it was to blame physical discomfort for our lack of happiness!

When 'what is' is resisted then more suffering is created. There is a constant, underlying dissatisfaction, otherwise known as the 'If only…' syndrome: if only this, that or the other happened, then I could be happy / if only so-and-so would change his or her behavior then I could be happy / if only I had more money or had a good lover, then I could be happy. The list is endless. You can fill in the blanks for yourself.

Accepting what is, as it is, doesn't mean that we become like a doormat and get walked over by all and sundry. Rather, it means recognizing that what happened even just a second ago can never be changed. It is letting the past be where it is so it doesn't take over the future.

But Dharma Tan wasn't just asking us if we were happier. He was teaching us that the very purpose is to find the inner peace that is our deepest joy. He was saying that there is enough pain and suffering in the world already, that the very nature of life includes change, unfulfilled desires, and a longing for things to be different than how they are, all of which brings discontent and dissatisfaction.

Our monk was constantly emphasizing that through meditation we could find a deeper contentment, one that is independent of anything or anyone but arises naturally within.

From this place of inner cheerfulness, we awaken kindness. There is a reservoir of basic goodness in all beings but, although it is an innate part of us, we often lose touch with this natural expression of caring and friendship. It's as if we get caught in quicksand, drawn or pulled into situations that cause discomfort.

"Meditation is calming the reptilian brain," says theologian **Matthew Fox**. "We have three brains in us: one is a reptilian brain, which is about 420 million years old; our mammal brain is half that old; and our most recent one is the intellectual creative brain.

"We have to calm the reptilian brain so that the mammal brain, which is here to bring kindness, kinship and bonding, can function. I mean, reptiles do not make good lovers; that is not their thing.

"Meditation allows us to treat the reptilian brain well: 'Nice crocodile, nice crocodile.' When we calm the crocodile, then the mammal brain can assert itself."

In meditation we meet ourselves as we are, neuroses and all, and as the experience deepens so too does our perception. As the heart opens we bring acceptance to our fallibilities and humanness. From embracing ourselves with kindness, such warmth then grows to embrace others.

In this way, meditation has the effect of lifting us out of the quicksand, out of misunderstanding and suffering. Through it we find freedom from reactive and self-serving behavior. It is the most compassionate gift we can give to ourselves.

We Are Not Who We Think We Are

Perhaps you have heard this story about a frog and a scorpion:

One day a frog was sitting happily by the side of the river when a scorpion came along.

"Oh Mr. Frog," said the scorpion, "I need to get to the other side of the river to be with my family. Will you please carry me across?"

"But Mr. Scorpion, if I do that, then you will sting me!" replied the frog, somewhat aghast at the request.

"No, I won't," said the scorpion.

"Do you promise?" asked a rather doubtful frog.

"I really promise—I will not sting you," assured the scorpion.

"Do you really, really promise?" asked a still dubious frog.

"Yes, I *really* promise," replied the scorpion, very sincerely.

"Okay," the frog said reluctantly. "Hop on."

The scorpion climbed on top of the frog's back and they set off. Halfway across the river, the scorpion stung the frog. In horror, unable to continue swimming and with both of them about to drown, the frog managed to gasp:

"Please, Mr. Scorpion, just tell me one thing before we both go under. Just tell me why, when you promised you wouldn't, why oh why did you sting me?"

"Because it is my nature to sting," replied the scorpion.

With no intention of being derogatory to scorpions, this story shows how its nature appears unchangeable, even fixed. A scorpion has no choice regarding its behavior because it is a scorpion; that's simply the way it is.

And most of us think we are just the same, we are the way we are and that's that, this is who I am and I won't change! But while a scorpion is not necessarily able to act any differently, we can. We do have choices. In the nineteenth century, philosopher William James said, "The great discovery of my generation is that a human being can alter his life by altering his attitudes."

So what keeps us locked in self-centeredness, stuck in small-mindedness and habitual patterns, unable to make any changes within ourselves? Could it be the ego, the most talked about yet least understood of all our human features?

The ego gives us a strong sense of self; it is the "me" part. This is neither good nor bad, except when self-centeredness dominates our thoughts, feelings, and perceptions. A positive sense of self gives us confidence and purpose, but a more negative sense makes us think we are the worst at everything. A selfish ego is unconcerned with other people's feelings, it thrives on the idea of me-first and impels us to cry out, "What about me? What about my feelings?"

"I think I'm the most important being in the world, but nobody else thinks it's about me, time doesn't think it's about me, the planet doesn't think it's about me, space doesn't think it's about me," says Professor **Robert Thurman**. "It doesn't take much to get the message that it's actually not about me. But if somebody comes and steps on my toe or wants to take away my strawberries, then suddenly it's all about me again!"

By watching how we equate ourselves with images of who we think we are, or with labels that reinforce that image and make us appear special, so the many manifestations of the ego appear: I am an American, Russian, Christian, Muslim; I am a teacher, doctor, divorcee, recovering alcoholic, etc. We hide behind our labels and become attached to the storyline they create, even introducing ourselves as a label, or only relating to others who have a similar one. Seeing through these illusions and being willing to give up our story is no small step.

"There is such pressure to keep each of my identities, each of my labels intact," writes **Joan Tollifson** in *Bare-Bones Meditation.* "Why do I feel as if no one really knows me until they know my story? Tremendous fear arises at the thought of losing my labels, and at the same time there is immense peace in living without them."

The nature of the ego is to stay in control, so it does all it can to keep us in the realm of "me-ness." It is a remarkably good shape shifter and can take any number of disguises or appear in many varied forms. For instance, it can make us believe we are the cleverest, the best informed and most important, as easily as it can make us feel unworthy, unlovable, and definitely not good enough to be happy.

"I gave up acting so I could be real," says actor **Linus Roache**. "Actors are inherently full of pretense, self-centeredness and narcissism, and I wanted to be more authentic.

"Until I realized that it's not just actors who are full of ego, everybody is! Everybody has their layers of pre-tenses and images of who they think they are. I finally saw that acting was not the problem; rather it was my relationship to it that mattered. I could actually be a real, authentic person who also happened to act. Without access to the inner dimensions of freedom, I can't be either an actor or a fully authentic person."

Self-centeredness and selfishness—the hallmarks of the ego—affect not only our relationships but also our behavior in the world. There is no limit to the damage a strong ego can do, from the arrogant conviction that its own opinions are the only right ones and everyone should be made to believe in them, to wielding and abusing power.

Theoretically, all that is needed is we let go of the focus on 'me', on the sense of separateness, the need for distinction, the grasping and clinging to the story. But this is far easier said than done!

"If we don't understand other people's feelings, their suffering or behavior, then we are only concerned with our own ego and image," says spiritual teacher **Mingyur Rinpoche**. "If the ego gets too strong, then it causes anxiety, depression, anger, jealousy, or insecurity. Then our ego becomes even bigger in order to protect us. We think that to defeat others is the only way to survive: 'I have to be tough in order to reach my goals.'"

This brings us to the importance of meditation. Without such a practice of self-reflection, we are subject to the ego's every whim and have no way of putting a brake on its demands. Meditation, on the other hand, gives us the space to see ourselves clearly and objectively, a place from which we can witness our behavior so that the ego's influence can be reduced.

In India, a coconut is traditionally offered to the guru as a sign of the student's willingness to surrender his or her ego and self-obsession, because a coconut is the hardest nut to crack. Such a symbolic gesture shows how the ego is considered to be a huge obstacle to self-growth and an even greater impediment to developing qualities like loving kindness and compassion.

However, such altruistic aspects emerge the more we meditate, while the self-centered and egotistic ones begin to diminish. As the need to be constantly engaged in our own storyline loses its importance, so the ego releases its grip and becomes less demanding. In this way, it soon becomes redundant, out of a job, irrelevant, and no longer an issue.

The ego also makes us believe that we are the dust on the mirror and could never be so beautiful as the radiant reflection beneath the surface. Yet how extraordinary to believe that we couldn't be so luminous when such resplendence is our true nature! As meditation increases awareness and reduces a sense of self-importance, so it enables us to merge with our true nature, free of impediments.

We began this with a story of a scorpion stinging the frog, so that both the frog and the scorpion drown. This story demonstrates how fixed and self-absorbed we can become, even to the point of jeopardizing our own wellbeing. But we have also seen how mindfulness and meditation can transform this self-centeredness by opening the heart.

Now the choice arises whether to offer generosity instead of selfishness, kindness instead of malice, and harmlessness instead of harm. To illustrate this, here is the end of the story:

> Two monks were washing their bowls in the river when they noticed a scorpion that was drowning. One monk immediately scooped it up and set it upon the bank. In the process, he was stung.
>
> He went back to washing his bowl, and again the scorpion fell in the river. Again the monk saved the scorpion, and again he was stung.
>
> Incredulously, the other monk asked him, "Friend, why do you continue to save the scorpion when you know its nature is to sting?"
>
> "Because," the monk replied, "it is my nature to save."

Why Meditation Can Seem So Difficult

What is it about something as simple as sitting still and watching our breath that evokes panic or even fear? No matter how many reports there are proving the mental, emotional and physical value of meditation, there seems to be a greater number of people who resist it.

No doubt meditation can be challenging; it can seem very odd to just sit there listening to the incessant chatter in our heads. Without entertainment we easily get bored.

After years of hearing a plethora of reasons why people find it hard to meditate, we've whittled it down to just a few.

1. *I'm too busy, I don't have the time.* Which can certainly be true if you have young children or a full-time job. However, we are only talking about five minutes a day. It may appear like we don't have time because we fill every minute with activities without ever pressing the pause button.

2. *I find it really uncomfortable.* If you are trying to sit cross-legged on the floor then, yes, it can get uncomfortable. But try sitting upright in a chair instead. Or do moving meditation like walking, yoga or tai chi.

3. *My mind can't stop thinking.* As you get quiet you find all this noisy chatter going on in your mind. This chatter is always there but you're usually unaware of it. Now you are. Meditation is not about stopping your thoughts, but becoming aware of them.

4. *There are too many distractions.* Gone are the days when we could disappear into a cave and remerge later, fully enlightened. But—and it's a big but—you needn't let distractions bother you. Cars going by outside? Fine. Let them go by, just don't go with them. The quiet you are looking for is inside you, not outside.

5. *I don't see the benefit.* Unfortunately, you'll have to take our word for this. Some people get the benefits of meditation after just one session, but most of us need longer. It might take you a week or more of daily practice. Which means you have to trust us enough to hang in there and keep going.

6. *I'm no good at this; I never get it right.* Actually, it's impossible to get it wrong. There are as many forms of meditation as there are people who practice it, so all you need do is find what works for you. Make friends with meditation, it's to be enjoyed!

7. *It's all just weird New Age hype.* Meditation is as old as the hills. Each religion has its own variation on the theme, all going back over many centuries, way before new age ideas began. So nothing new here, and nothing weird or whacky.

2 The Distress of Stress

Being Pulled Too Tight

Does your mother-in-law make you want to bite your nails? Does your work make you feel overwhelmed and unable to cope? Do you get burnt out, resentful or irritated? Do you keep loosing your temper? What do you do when you just want to scream and stop the world?

Imagine you are a caveman out with fellow tribe members on a hunt for food. You have spotted a large bear and adrenalin is beginning to pump through your body in anticipation of the coming hunt. As you close in on the animal your heart rate increases, breaths get shorter, stomach muscles tighten, and concentration deepens. The next few moments are crucial in determining whether you fight to the kill or run to the hills.

Now imagine a day when everything is too much to cope with. Perhaps your child has kept you awake all night with a toothache, you have to be at a business meeting first thing in the morning but you get delayed in congested traffic, the meeting goes on longer than planned and you have to skip lunch in order to write a report. An angry client then arrives demanding better service, just as your mother calls in need of help with her car.

In the midst of all this you may not have noticed that your heart rate was increasing, your breath was getting shorter, and your stomach muscles tightening as your anxiety level went up. Adrenalin is pumping through your body, but in this case there's no bear to fight and nowhere to run. Although separate incidents may appear benign, if your response to them becomes increasingly uptight then the body puts out the red alert.

If stress increases you become less able to adequately adapt, causing you to overreact, lose a clear perspective on priorities, get muddled or disorganized, become depressed, or rant and rage for no apparent reason. You may have more anxiety and panic, irritability and frustration, debilitating fear, insecurity, rapid mood changes, addictive behavior, or paranoia and confusion. And all of these are just a few of the possible effects. It's like a steam cooker coming to full pressure. You are the only one who can turn down the heat, but often feel powerless to do so.

Yet such states are considered normal! We proclaim, "My mind is driving me crazy!" as if this were some sort of achievement. If we continue to believe our issues are real then the dramas will get played out over and again.

"I was the guy who at forty-two years old had all the money I could ever spend," says educator **Jeff Salzman**. "I had the most beautiful husband imaginable, I was living in a beach house in Florida with my library of books. I really had nothing to worry about, and so I ended up with the only thing I had left: the fact that one day I was going to die.

"So I started worrying about my heart and went and got a blood pressure machine. Within three or four weeks I was taking my blood pressure forty to fifty times a day. This obsessive compulsive disorder continued to spiral for the next four years to the point where I was in a low level of panic all the time, with super-high blood pressure and heart arrhythmias. I couldn't sleep; I couldn't concentrate on anything. I was stressed to the max, but it was entirely my own doing."

An experience such as Jeff's shows how easily a pattern of thinking can become a full-blown neurosis. Not me, you think, I don't get stressed! Perhaps not, but imagine you are squeezing some toothpaste out of a tube but you've forgotten to take the cap off. What happens? Deb did this in one of her most unaware moments (they do happen!), and the toothpaste soon found another way out—through the bottom of the tube and onto her clothes.

Now imagine that the tube of toothpaste is you under pressure and beginning to experience psychological or emotional distress. But you don't take the cap off, as it were, by recognizing what is happening and making time to relax and deal with your concerns. Instead, you just keep squeezing yourself to do more.

So what happens to the mental or emotional pressure building up inside? Eventually it has to find a way out and if it can't come out through the top—by being acknowledged, expressed and resolved—then it'll come out through the body and mind.

It will find the weakest point, whether through eating patterns, the digestive system, nerves, immune system, behavior, emotional balance, or sleep patterns. Repressed or ignored it becomes illness, depression, addiction, or anxiety; projected outward, it becomes hostility, aggression, prejudice, or fear. But all of this is within our own personal domain.

"When I'm working in corporations, I ask how many people get stressed by traffic and most people say yes, traffic jams definitely make me stressed," says author **Peter Russell**. "Yet sitting in a traffic jam is the least stressful part of driving! We have nothing to do, nobody is demanding anything from us; it's actually a moment when we can completely relax.

"So why do we get so stressed? Is it because we feel out of control? Are we going to be late for a meeting and will then be criticized or lose an opportunity? It's the voice that wants to be in control of things that is stressing us out, not the traffic jam."

Stress is a derivation of a Latin word meaning *to be drawn tight*, which is exactly what is happening. Job dissatisfaction, moving, divorce and financial difficulties lie at the top of the list of known stressors that make us tighten up. But we all respond differently to such circumstances. For instance, a divorce may seem to be a high stressor but for some it can be a welcome relief. The difference is in our response to the stressor, for although we may have little or no control over the circumstances we are dealing with, we do have control over our reaction to them.

"I was 17 years old and on my first ten-day Zen meditation retreat," recalls **Deb**. "Each day we had work assignments, but there never seemed to be enough time to do the whole job before the next meditation session began. On one occasion I started to panic. I was trying to finish weeding a flowerbed and I couldn't, I got totally stressed out, it all just got too much and I burst into tears.

"The teacher, Jiyu Kennet Roshi, came over to me. Very gently she said, 'You can never have too much to do. You just do what is in front of you, and when you are finished, you do the next thing.' This radically changed my attitude toward work!"

The immediate cause of stress is not being in the present moment; you are anywhere but here. The deeper cause of stress is the perception of our circumstances as being overwhelming, and our perception of our ability to cope when stretched beyond what we think we are capable. If we believe we can't cope, then we will begin to lose ground; if we believe we can cope, then we'll be able to ride over any obstacles.

There is no medical cure that can alleviate stress, no prescription drug that can lighten our workload or change our life conditions.

Luckily, we can transform our beliefs and our perceptions. The idea that it is our circumstances that are causing the stress and that if they were changed then we would be fine is seeing the situation from the wrong perspective. Rather, the belief that circumstances are causing the stress is what is actually causing the stress.

> "Meditation is staying conscious of one of the most important things to stay conscious of, and that's my internal programming in this moment," says educator **Marshall Rosenberg**.
>
> "There are four things that tell me it is time to meditate: depression, anger, guilt, and shame. When I stop, I can see what I am telling myself and I can translate this life-alienated, violence-provocative thinking into a life-serving consciousness and communication."

Although changing our circumstances certainly may help, invariably, no matter what we do, it is a change within our perception of our capabilities that will make the biggest difference. In turn, this will help develop the relaxation response and begin to normalize everything the stress response has put out of balance.

Medication v Meditation

For fast-acting relief, try slowing down. Lily Tomlin

Most of us think of relaxation as putting our feet up, having a beer, watching a good movie, walking the dog, or perhaps joining a fitness club. Certainly these activities help but too often they only deal with superficial, immediate aspects of stress. They make us feel better until the next deadline or traffic jam begins to push us over the edge again. To make more lasting changes we need to release unconscious levels of stress, as accumulated tension and resistance affect both behavior and health.

The power of thought is such that if we think we are getting stressed or overwhelmed, we are more likely to induce the stress response. In the same way, if we think easeful and relaxing thoughts, we will induce the relaxation response.

"Usually, when we feel the pressure of life then we can become very tense and close our heart. We go into a state of self-protection and self-preservation. When our mind can become calm and more spacious, then we see there is nothing to worry about," says spiritual teacher **Ponlop Rinpoche.**

"The greatest warrior in history is the one who is calm. If he freaked out then he would easily lose the battle. In the same way, when our mind is stressed and tense, we think everyone is attacking us and we can't see anyone objectively or lovingly.

"Meditation really helps us not to panic or freak out; it brings us back to this calm ground where we can see ourselves clearly."

In a stressed state it is easy to be irritated or overwhelmed by relatively small events—a child interrupting our conversation or a colleague being late for a meeting—until we become uptight or tense. When the relaxation response kicks in, conflicting situations can be handled without a red flag waving, adrenalin being released, feelings of fear, anxiety, or hopelessness. In a relaxed state, such disturbances are seen for what they are; we are more likely to be concerned as to why our colleague is late than focusing on the inconvenience.

> "I came across a definition of meditation that it comes from the root meaning 'right balance.' That rang true for me because, personally, my attention is often so fragmented, egocentric, narcissistic, or self-concerned that there isn't a whole lot of balance going on," says inspirational teacher **Joan Borysenko**. "Right balance is when my mind isn't spinning out endless movies and delusions, or maybe it still is but I'm just not so attached to believing them.
>
> "Meditation is when I can watch stuff go by and the part of me that usually interrupts and says, 'That's a good story,' or 'That son of a bitch,' or 'I'm guilty and awful,' that part sits back and sees it as just another story. This gives me the most delicious sense of spaciousness and ease."

Mindfulness enables us to pay attention when our breathing becomes shorter or there's a tightening of the abdominal muscles, when a headache develops, when we get short-tempered, or there is a growing hopelessness. Such awareness recognizes when our perception of ourselves may be limiting our behavior or making us more susceptible to prevailing pressures.

The words *medication* and *meditation* are both derived from the Latin word *medicus*, meaning to care or to cure, indicating that both mindfulness and meditation are the most appropriate medicines for stress. The ability to keep our peace and maintain an even-balanced state is one of the greatest gifts that we can bring to any situation.

> "I would have these adrenaline rushes as if I were nervous about something—kind of a low-grade anxiety attack—and then I would immediately start to get anxious," says yoga teacher **Cyndi Lee**. "It would get all blown up in my mind. By meditating with it, I learned to recognize that I didn't need to go into drama queen mental mode, I could just let this be, let it rise and let it pass."

In practice, this means recognizing there are many moments where we have no control over what happens, no ability to affect the outcome, but whatever happens it is possible to stay balanced. This applies to thoughts and feelings as well as to our behavior and actions. As the German proverb says, *We can't direct the wind, but we can adjust our sails.*

This sense of detachment from what is happening is huge. It's not a cold, uncaring, unfeeling detachment; it's just taking a step backwards. We see what is happening but don't *become* what is happening. Meditation enables us to be with what is if the stress response is kicking in or adrenalin is influencing our reactions, rather than over-identifying with the stress. Mindfulness empowers us to be present and observe; by witnessing we are no longer dominated by reactive or knee-jerk behavior.

> "Whether referred by their physician or not, people come with a huge amount of pain and suffering, both physical and emotional," says mindfulness teacher **Jon Kabat-Zinn**.
>
> "Through the cultivation of mindfulness they develop a more functional relationship with that suffering, they turn towards it, open to it, and actually befriend

it, rather than insisting that it stop; in the process the pain often transforms or even falls away.

"For the most part, they will tell you they are more in touch with their own beauty than they have been since they were children. It is jaw-dropping."

Such equanimity gives strength and a sense of being unshakable in a world that is constantly demanding and challenging. The movement is from fear and chaos into awareness of the bigger picture. We can never know what is going to happen or when, nothing is predictable, permanent, secure, controllable, or dependable. Life never stands still, no matter what we do— evolution does not go backwards. Change is the very nature of existence, like rain and sunshine, or night and day. What a relief! Just imagine if everything were permanent—there would be no butterflies, no full moon, no cherry blossoms and no cherries.

However, it is in those very moments when everything looks hopeless that we have a real chance to grow into something better; what the caterpillar calls the end of the world, we call a butterfly!

We can ignore the reality of change and live with the delusion of permanency and predictability, or we can embrace impermanence and unpredictability with awareness and dignity.

Stress and Illness

We tend to take our physical bodies very much for granted and our health even more so. As a result, when something goes wrong it can be alarming, even frightening. We ask, "Why is this happening to me?" as if we had been walking around inside a stranger.

The more stressed we become, the more our breathing becomes rapid, short, and shallow, and the more we ignore our physical needs. In other words, we get stuck in our heads and become increasingly ungrounded.

The mind and body are in continual and intimate communication, the body often expressing the denied, ignored or repressed parts of the mind: as we think so we have become, and as we have become so we can see how we have been thinking.

> "When I feel stressed, then I sit in meditation and ask myself, 'Where in my body am I feeling it?' Often it's in my gut, or some place of holding," says publisher **Tami Simon.** "I say, 'Okay, you don't have to hold onto anything, your chair is supporting you, and the earth is supporting you.'
>
> "Then I can literally sink down into the earth. I feel my feet get heavy, I feel my hands open up, I feel my back get heavy and drop, and then I start dropping my energy. It is a deep relaxation. I am no longer in my mind, but I'm sinking into both my body and the ground."

By meditating with awareness of the body we can begin to unravel the emotional and psychological patterns that have developed.

We can hear what the held places are saying, what issues are being ignored, and what is needed to bring a deeper release. As Christine Evans describes in Deb's book, *Your Body Speaks Your Mind:*

> "I try to just notice myself, without judgment. I notice that I feel sick when my ex-lover rings, I notice that I feel sad when my lower back is massaged," says bodyworker **Christine Evans**. "I notice the area between my shoulder blades that aches when I'm feeling tense. I notice the sick feeling, the retching and vomiting, is about not accepting how I really feel and not believing that I have the right to feel it."

Often it is easier to see the connection between stress and mindfulness, than to see it when we are very sick, perhaps dealing with issues such as cancer or AIDS. At such times we may be more prone to feeling self-pity, helplessness and dependency. Yet meditation not only reduces stress-related physical problems, but it can move us out of negative mindsets so that we can be more at peace with whatever is happening.

> "We started an AIDS clinic at the very beginning of the epidemic and it was truly remarkable to watch people go from a place of feeling they were a passive victim of something that is going to kill them to a place of inquiry, to asking, 'What can I learn about myself?'" says inspirational teacher **Joan Borysenko**.
>
> "I remember one man in particular, Mark, this young twenty-eight-year-old handsome gay guy with a great job and a great life who looked at me and said, 'I never thought I would say this, but I can't imagine what my life would have been like without AIDS because I would never have come to this level of self-discovery or inner peace.'"

Our dear friend Mark Matousek was that young man. His memory of that time is one of transforming his worry and fear into a powerful inner strength.

"Mortality led me to meditation," says author **Mark Matousek**. "Being diagnosed with a then-terminal disease at age 28, I was forced to pursue an inner life as a survival mechanism. I felt compelled to discover if there was anything beyond this booby-trapped bag of bones.

"By sitting and watching my breath, by learning to sit *through* bad moments, a metaphysical muscle seemed to strengthen in the stillness. Running from pain or fear made the badness worse, whereas when I stopped in the midst of it all, took my seat, and let the feelings burn through me, clarity slowly took the place of hysteria. Meditation was a place to empty out, grieve, and refill, to stop and be still.

"That was thirty-plus years ago. My health crisis passed but the practice stayed. Meditation is on my shoulder, a reminder of beauty, truth, fragility, sorrow; a voice that whispers: 'Remember to love.' If my outer world had not been so threatened I would never have looked for an inner one."

Acknowledging vulnerabilities, emotional trauma, and psychological or physical pain is not that simple, especially as our usual response to pain is to make it go away by whatever means possible. Instead, in the stillness of meditation, we can gently enter into the pain by letting go of resistance, as well as all the ways we have held on and what we have been holding on to.

Illness can make us feel limited by or locked in the body, our behavior and actions determined by what we can and cannot do. But rather than getting lost in the story, we can develop greater objectivity. And when we don't identify with the story, the diagnosis or prognosis, the details or the dramas, we are free to expand into our true potential. This can eventually lead to a deep gratitude for what the illness is teaching us.

Deb has MS, and as we were working on this book she would be in her wheelchair at her desk, writing.

> "Mindfulness informs me when I resist what's happening in my body," says **Deb**. "If I resist then I suffer, so I breathe into the restrictions and the physical changes, and the resistance softens. Meditation reminds me that there may be discomfort but I don't need to become it. Who I am inside is not the discomfort."

Some years ago the much-loved American teacher Ram Dass had a stroke. He told us how he'd always been fiercely independent, so one of his first lessons was becoming dependent on others, which he's come to see as a huge blessing.

> "Meditation gives me purchase on the stroke; it teaches me I am that I am awareness," says spiritual teacher **Ram Dass**. "It frees me from identification with the limitations of the stroke."

Becoming aware leads to a deeper acceptance and healing of ourselves. We can't accept something we are unaware of and we can't become aware without paying attention, watching, and listening. In this sense, meditation is both medicine and healing, a bringing together of the different aspects of ourselves into a unified whole.

We witness what is happening in the body without becoming the illness; we may be physically limited but can remain unlimited within ourselves.

3 Growing Roses Out of Compost: Desire, Anger and Fear

The Dragons In Our Mind

Soon after his release, Nelson Mandela was asked by Bill Clinton if he was feeling angry the day he walked away from 27 years in jail. "Tell me the truth, when you were walking to freedom that last time, didn't you hate them?" Clinton asked, referring to Mandela's jailors. "You must have been so angry!"

"Sure I was," Mandela replied. "I felt great anger and hatred and bitterness. But I also knew that if I continued hating then once I got in that car and out through the gate I would still be in prison. I let it go because I wanted to be free."

Such awareness as Mandela displayed is rare. Normally, we don't accept or release our negative feelings so easily. Rather, we repress or disown them. But these sentiments are ignored at our peril, for when denied they may cause guilt, shame, depression, relationship failure, rage, or sadness. When recognized, such hidden places contain great resources of strength, for locked in the darkness is a depth of sensitivity and insight.

"Our hang-ups, unfortunately or fortunately, contain our wealth," writes spiritual teacher **Pema Chödron** in *The Wisdom of No Escape*. "Our neurosis and our wisdom are made out of the same material. If you throw out your neurosis, you also throw out your wisdom."

To run or hide from the obstacles that confront us—the dragons in our mind—simply increases resistance, making us a casualty of ourselves. Awareness of our dark corners can be the impetus that brings greater self-reflection. From knowing the darkness comes the urge to grow into a strong and healed self, like a weed impelled to grow through concrete in order to reach the light.

Can mindfulness and meditation help us embrace and accept our essential humanness? We have seen how they are the appropriate remedies for stress and illness, but can the same be said of more psychological states, such as greed, anger or fear? How do we deal with the shadow issues that invariably arise during a self-reflective practice?

"When I met my shadow right in front of my face, I knew that spirit was saying, 'Honey, if you want to heal yourself, you've got to walk right into this fire. This is your shadow, and this is what is keeping you from self-love. You are not going to be of any service to this world unless you go right into it and find out who that little girl in you is,'" says yoga teacher **Seane Corn**.

"If I can come to terms with the parts of myself that scare me, then when I meet them I can say, 'Oh, I get it, you're my teacher, you're going to kick my ass on a psychic level in order to open my heart.'"

Growing up with an abusive or absent parent, in poverty, or with little emotional stability are just some of the ways emotional dysfunction manifests. When this happens, we have three choices: to perpetuate the same type of behavior in our own life, to ignore or deny our feelings so that we live without really knowing ourselves, or to use the experience as a means for transformation.

"One of my most painful childhood experiences is of my father and I having an argument," recalls **Ed**. "He was in the bedroom with the door closed, and by playing outside the door I had disturbed him. When I was angrily told to be quiet, like any kid I shouted back, 'I didn't ask to be born!' Little did I know this would trigger a huge reaction: my father came flying out of the room and nearly attacked me.

"Later, I came to understand that he must have felt responsible for making my mother pregnant and, therefore, for her death so soon after my birth. So much power was in both of our shadow minds."

As long as places we have hidden from stay in the dark, they will continue to dominate our behavior. Only by exploring their true nature and accepting that they are a part of being alive can we bring real transformation. Meditation enables us to meet these places. As we touch into levels of grief or shame, repressed anger or hidden fear, in the touching is a knowing of ourselves in a fuller way. We are more complete, as if something lost has finally been found.

We taught meditation in a men's prison in England, and the experience was as transformative for us as it was for the inmates. In exploring and expressing their own dark places, the men saw how easy it is to become literally locked into avoidance or denial. Through meditation, they began to realize that rather than looking outside for freedom they could find it within themselves. Until then, as Bo Lozoff of the Prison Ashram Project says, we are all doing time, whether in jail or not.

"I was seventeen years old and was in jail for maybe the twelfth time; I thought I was probably going to prison for a really long time for robbery, drugs, you name it, I'd done it," says meditation teacher **Noah Levine.** "I had all of the suffering from the past—the shame, guilt, and regret, the anger, vengeance, and resentment—all were playing out in my head.

"At that point something started screaming inside me: 'This isn't everyone else's fault! You're the one taking the drugs! You're the one committing the crimes! You're the one doing the same thing over and over and expecting it to be different!'

"Then my father called me and he said, 'Why don't you try meditation?' I had no answer, no reason not to. I'd already tried everything else.

"The immediate result was relief. One breath at a time. Half a breath at a time. The only thing that I've ever done that has ever worked is meditation, it's the only place where I've found any real reprieve. It helped me see that anger or fear is just what happens when we get into certain situations: anger arises, fear arises, sadness comes. Meditation enabled me to take such negativity less personally and, perhaps more importantly, to meet it with more care and compassion."

Desire And Addiction

We have times of great joy, wonder, laughter and sharing in our lives. But there are also times when we are not so nice, when we treat each other in ways that belie our sociability: we are attacked for being a different religion or color, women and children are raped and abused, while huge numbers are homeless and hungry.

So why do we see others who are different from us as the enemy? Why do we project our hidden fears onto them so that they become the problem that needs to be annihilated, rather than recognizing the intolerance within ourselves? Can we not see that our ego-bound selfishness and desire for things to be different is a major cause of our disregard for each other?

Desire has many aspects, such as selfishness, greed, covetousness, or addiction. It is most obvious when we see land becoming more important than people, leaving people homeless; when medicines are kept away from those who need them because the price is too high; or when crops are grown to sell while workers go hungry. But the same traits are also found in our own families when divided by disagreements, or in ourselves when our need for the next fix is stronger than our self-control. We rarely reach out beyond our own self-interested comfort zone.

Deb was attending a meditation group led by Tibetan teacher Lama Chime Rinpoche at his center, Marpa House in England, when a man at the back of the room spoke up.

The man said: "I don't want to keep meditating. Because I know that if I keep meditating then I'll stop wanting things, and I don't want to stop wanting things."

Chime Rinpoche roared with laughter. He replied, "Look at me. I've been meditating a very long time but I still want things. I still want good food to eat and clean clothes to wear; I want a warm house, and I want to be with my wife and family.

"The difference is, if I don't get these things then it doesn't matter."

The myth that the grass is greener elsewhere is one we live by for vast amounts of our waking time—the underlying searching, yearning and longing to fulfill the latest need, for circumstances to be other than they are.

There is a hidden irony to all this, which is that nothing stays the same, neither the yearning nor the object of the desire. The world around us has already changed from just a moment ago. Somewhere leaves have fallen, babies have been born, clouds have passed overhead. Who we are now is not who we were last year, last week, yesterday, even a minute ago; already our wants and desires have changed. Our needs are here one minute and gone the next.

Giving up addiction means changing myself? Really? This fear of change tries to make everything appear solid and everlasting. However, as impermanence is a reality, when we resist it we are resisting the very meaning of our being here, which is to always be evolving or becoming something more than we were before.

"In the smallest, quietest ways, impermanence feels like the ground of my being, more beautiful and awe inspiring than scary," says author **Mark Matousek.** "The part of the mind that sees itself during meditation is not afraid of impermanence any more than fish are scared of water. It is only the part of the mind that can't swim—fear, clinging, self-obsession, control—that sinks, defeated by the truth of transience."

The experience of sitting in quiet reflection enables us to see the urgency of desire, how insatiable our needs are, and how craving and addiction can run our lives. And while meditation does not leave us free of needs, it does free us from the desire to fulfill those needs. Then greed, or the wanting and longing for things to be different, can become appreciation for what we have.

"I was a Harvard playboy and I loved the theater and drinking and dancing on tables and going to Mexico; at the same time, I was seriously reading books about awakening and enlightenment," says Professor **Robert Thurman**.

"I used to race sports cars, and I was changing a tire when the rim flipped the tire iron into my eye. When I woke up they had taken it out.

"Losing my eye meant I gained a thousand eyes into the deep visceral value of impermanence, what in Tibet is called the immediacy of death, meaning that death is here with us right now. That insight shaped all my subsequent experiences."

Take a moment now to appreciate the chair you are sitting on as you read this. Consider what went into the making of this chair: the wood, cotton, wool, or other fibers, the trees and plants that were used, the animals that were involved and maybe gave their lives, the earth that grew the trees and plants, the sun and rain, the people who prepared the materials, the factory where the chair was made, the designer and carpenter and seamstress, the shop and the people that sold the chair—all this just so you could be sitting here now.

There is no beginning place. If we pull on a single thread in nature, we find it is attached to the rest of the world. No part of our being is separate or independent from anything else, there is just an endless stream of connectedness linking everything together. And we think we have nothing to feel grateful for!

> "We were in Australia on our honeymoon, and I wanted to show Deb what a great body surfer I was," recalls **Ed**. "So I strode into the waves and swam out beyond the breakers. But suddenly I was being pulled by a strong undertow. No matter how hard I struggled, I was going nowhere. I tried to stay centered amidst the rising panic until, finally, by swimming diagonally to one side, I managed to inch my way back to the shore.
>
> "Deb, of course, knew nothing of my struggles. She just saw this bedraggled show-off limping back along the beach. But the gratitude, the appreciation, the joy of being alive was far greater than my battered ego! Everything was suddenly so vivid and precious; the sand beneath my feet felt like gold dust."

In meditation we may spontaneously experience tremendous gratitude. We don't feel grateful *to* something but grateful *for* something, for its very existence, for the fact that it exists at all. Gratitude is then transformed into generosity, the antidote to self-centeredness and greed. It is a natural movement from self to other.

You may think that one person's generosity doesn't make a real difference. But even small gestures can have a very big impact—consider how much of an affect a single mosquito can have! It is the act of giving itself that is important. As Gandhi said, "Almost anything we do will seem insignificant, but it is very important that we do it."

Getting Underneath Anger

Some people are always grumbling because roses have thorns. I am thankful that thorns have roses. Alphonse Karr

None of us want to admit that we get irritated, bitchy, or lose our temper. We much prefer to think of ourselves as wonderfully tolerant and serene.

But anger has many faces. It can appear as irritation, frustration, rage, even hatred, while repressed anger may become depression or hostility. Anger can dominate and control our behavior, condemning everything as wrong except itself. It has been described as a single match that can burn down an entire forest.

"I have done anger and I have harmed people; it has been done to me and I have been harmed. I see people acting out anger and thinking it's okay, but there's no awareness of the other person," says psychotherapist **Maura Sills.**

"I come from a family that was angry; it was the way we related to one another. I believed that if people had trouble with my anger, it was their problem, and I had a right to act the way I wanted. But when we express anger, we are creating more pain and suffering in ourselves, and what we do with it can cause so much damage."

There may be layers of conflicting feelings hidden beneath anger, such as hurt, insecurity, longing, or fear, all trying to be heard. The power of rage means that it can act as a defense mechanism and overshadow these other emotions, causing us to lose touch with ourselves and then struggle to articulate what we are really feeling.

Having lost connectedness, anger may be expressing feelings of rejection, grief, loneliness, or a longing to be loved. It may actually be saying, "I love you" or "I need you," yet we are hurling abuse at each other instead.

If anger is repressed or denied then all these feelings become repressed and denied as well. As it takes over, anger leaves little room for awareness; our heart goes out of reach, while we lose contact with both our own feelings and those of the person we are mad at.

> "We get to see that underneath anger there is fear, pain and sorrow, and we can't deal with anger unless we also deal with what sustains it," says Rabbi **Zalman Schachter-Shalomi**.
>
> "We forget how we are hardwired. The reptilian system within us makes sure we are secure and safe. If we don't feel secure, then the dinosaur will rear its head and roar. So under anger is always the question of how safe does the reptile feel?"

Trying to eradicate anger is like trying to box with our own shadow: it doesn't work. Getting rid of it implies both expressing it and causing emotional damage, or repressing it until it becomes depression, when it erupts at a later time causing even more harm. If we keep avoiding it, anger will keep running after us. Feeling guilty for getting angry is just adding more suffering to an already painful situation: "So you got angry, okay!"

Identifying with anger as "my" anger makes it solid, real, and justified; the ego is asserting itself. Owning anger makes it stay around longer than it needs to, like a fly caught in fly-paper. Expressing anger brings pain to others; repressing it brings pain to ourselves. Instead there is a midpoint between expressing anger and repressing it. This middle place is where our feelings can be voiced but with awareness, both of our own feelings and of their effect.

> "Ducks don't do anger, they fight over a piece of bread and then they just swim away," says Hakomi therapist **Deepesh Faucheux**. "People keep processing everything that happens to them—what so and so did to me, how she wronged me, why doesn't he respect me—and this maintains anger and resentment. But if we can disconnect from the storyline that goes with the anger then we create a gap between reacting and responding."

In this way, as anger arises, we can stay present, keeping our heart open, breathing, watching emotions come up and pass through. We watch as anger fills our mind and makes a big song and dance, and we keep breathing as we watch it leave. We see the ego in action, honor the passion, and observe its destructive nature dissipate under the spotlight.

> "You are going to be angry when someone knocks your coffee all over you, or when they say you're a dork instead of saying how great you are," says Professor **Robert Thurman**.
> "But if you meditate on how fruitless and absolutely destructive anger is, then you may still get angry but you will get angry a little less. If I don't meditate, I can easily get frazzled. I was very hot-tempered as a young person and I'm not totally cured, I don't pretend to be a holy person, but I'm much freer of it now."

Only by recognizing the real emotion behind the anger can there be more honest communication. Meditation is very important here, in order to witness anger, get to know it, and even to make friends with it.

"When I first started meditating, I thought that all the things like anger would go away, but what I've found is that I'm the same person with the same habitual tendencies," says Professor **Judith Simmer-Brown**.

"I'm still prone to irritation and anger; I still have a hair-trigger temper. The difference is that I can allow space to feel the feeling. It's very much a part of who I am, but I'm not driven to act on it, I'm not compelled by it in the same way."

Meditation is not a cure-all. It's not going to make all our difficulties go away or suddenly transform our weaknesses into strengths, but it does enable us to rest in an inclusive acceptance of who we are. This doesn't make us perfect, simply more fully human.

"I still see anger arise, even after thirty years of meditation," says spiritual teacher **Ram Dass.** "But meditation has helped me to overcome the more negative places because it allows me not to identify with these states. For example, I am loving awareness and what I am aware of is anger."

Hanging Out With Fear

Where anger is hot and loud, fear is more subtle and pervasive. But it too possesses many different disguises. On the one hand, fear is a natural response to physical danger, but on the other it can be self-created, such as the fear of failure, of the dark, of being different, or of being lonely. We fear love because we fear being rejected, fear being generous because we fear scarcity, fear sharing our thoughts in case we appear wrong or stupid, and we fear our own beauty so we become riddled with self-doubt and insecurity.

"Fear is natural. Your body spent hundreds of thousands of years perfecting it," says psychologist **Gay Hendricks**. "It's normal; it's human. Breathe with it. Above all, don't tempt the universe by shaking a fist at fear and saying that you won't acknowledge its existence. That is like shaking your fist at thunder and saying you'll never listen to it again."

Self-generated fear is seen in its acronym: F.E.A.R. or False Evidence Appearing Real. It appears real even though it may have no real substance. It arises when the ego is threatened or undermined, making us cling to the known and familiar. Such fear creates nervous disorders and paranoia.

Fear can also make us wary of love and spontaneity, keeping us emotionally frozen, unable to move forward. In this way, it reinforces separateness and isolation, creating loneliness and enmity. The immediate effect is to shut us down and to shut off the heart.

Just for a moment, let your body take a position of feeling fearful. What is your posture? Most people hunch their shoulders forward, fold their arms across their chests, or assume a similarly contracted defensive pose that shields the heart. In this self-protective stance, the heart goes out of reach and it's impossible to feel love or even friendliness.

Now, while your arms are folded firmly across your heart, try saying, "I love you" with real meaning. Hard to do!

When fear is arising, we can use both mindfulness and the breath to stay receptive, breathing consciously into our heart area while naming the fear as fear. Watch what happens to the body as fear tries to take hold. As long as we can keep the body open and in a place of complete acceptance, it will be very hard for fear to establish itself.

> "The process of meditation is one of slowly peeling away our resistance and fear; there is a greater vulnerability, as well as an acceptance of the vulnerability," says entertainer **David Shiner.** "Rather than pushing that away and living within the walls of fear that the mind has created, we realize it's not going to hurt us, that it's actually a good thing. I can feel more deeply; I can trust the choices I make; there is gratitude."

Where fear closes the heart, love embraces it. So now try taking the posture of love. Watch how your body opens and expands, your arms reaching outward, inviting and accepting. Watch how your breathing gets deeper, fuller. Fear may still be there, but love can welcome and embrace it. Where fear shuts out love, love holds fear tenderly, like the sky that contains everything.

With your arms stretched wide, now try saying, "I'm fearful" and really mean it. Hard to do!

> "There's a world of love and there's a world of fear too and very often that fear feels a lot more real and certainly more urgent than the feeling of love," says

musician **Bruce Springsteen** to David Hepworth in The
"Q" Interview. "When that world of love comes rushing
in, a world of fear comes with it. To open yourself up
to love you've got to embrace the fear as well. It's about
walking through that world of fear so that you can live
in a world of love."

In other words, being fearless doesn't mean stopping or
denying the fear; it's not the same as being without fear. Rather,
fearlessness is fully feeling the fear, naming it, getting to know
it, and then going beyond it. Fear may stop us from facing our
demons and participating fully in life, but fearlessness gives us
the courage to greet the unknown. We become unshakable,
confident and joyful, with fear as an ally.

Fear comes—breathe and let go. Fear comes—breathe
and reassure the mind that all is well. Fear comes—replace
it with love.

As long as we deny fear, anger, jealousy, or any other emotion, we are not accepting and embracing ourselves. Whether
a thought or a feeling is either positive or negative makes no
difference, it is still an integral part of our being. To reject one
part is to remain in denial of the whole.

"I was riddled with a kind of existential longing, fear
and despair," says publisher **Tami Simon**. "I wasn't sure
that I belonged on the planet, that I would ever have a
place for myself, that I would find a way to fit in. I was
desperate and totally freaked out.

"When I started meditating, it was the first time I
felt any synchronization in my being, any rooting or
anchoring. I felt a sense of incredible, unlimited joy and
possibility. Suddenly I had a reason for my existence
and, in a sense, at that moment, my life was saved."

Meditation encourages us to get to know fear so it is no longer the enemy. We can begin to see the benefits of fear, the unexpected insights and flashes of understanding that move us into a deeper awareness. No longer denying fear, judging it, or being frightened by it, we can let all these feelings come and go.

"Meditation calms us sufficiently to grasp the way our mind moves into rage, jealousy, violence, sadness, abandonment, fear, all the stuff that keeps coming up like marsh gas from within," says author **Andrew Harvey**. "It helps ground us in the peace of our inner being so that we can embrace ourselves without being shattered. Instead, by knowing ourselves, we are more noble, generous, and compassionate."

Making Friends With Panic

"I had panic all through my childhood until I was 13. I grew up at the base of the Himalaya Mountains and I was afraid of snowstorms, avalanches, earthquakes, fire, and sometimes I was just afraid for no reason at all," says Tibetan Buddhist teacher **Mingyur Rinpoche**.

However, where most of us are overcome by fear or panic, or try to suppress it, Mingyur did something with panic that is exemplary. He made friends with it, turning his enemy into his friend.

"There are two ways we actually make panic worse. We say *Yes Sir* to it, or *Get Out*," says **Mingyur**. "If we say *Yes Sir* then we let it rule us and we do anything that the panic asks of us. But if we try to get rid of it by saying *Get Out*, then this makes it into the enemy. Either way, panic gets bigger and we are less able to cope.

"Awareness means seeing it, feeling it, and recognizing how panic is made up of many different pieces: physical sensations, emotions, fearful images, words or thoughts," he says. "Awareness is of all the pieces. If you aren't aware of them then you are a victim of them."

1. **Become aware of the panic**, of the different parts that make up panic, of the deeper reasons and causes, with no judgment of either good or bad, just awareness.
2. **To shift focus away from** *Yes Sir* or *Get Out* bring your breathing to your belly, away from the panic. Breathe in

slowly and deeply, filling the belly, then gently breathing out. Silently repeat, *Soft belly, quiet mind,* as you breathe.

Mingyur Rinpoche was just 13 years old when he discovered the transformative power of meditation. The more he practiced, the more he was able to be with the panic and not let it run his life.

"Meditation enabled me to witness myself. Normally, my busy mind ran the show by telling me to dread something and then to panic. Meditation gave me greater freedom of the mind," **Mingyur** says. "Panic pushed me into understanding myself more deeply, and it opened my heart so that I have greater understanding of others who are also suffering."

Nothing Stays The Same

"I bottomed out of my life with drug addiction," says author **Debbie Ford**. "I really thought I was all of my stories and dramas and limitations and insecurities and worries and fears. I used drugs to fill a deep hole inside. I was a bad user for about thirteen or fourteen years; I went through four different treatment centers. Eventually, I started to ask, 'Who am I? What am I doing here?'

"Meditation allowed me to see that I wasn't my story, I wasn't my pain or suffering, I wasn't my skinny legs. I give thanks every day that I was a drug addict. That hole that I felt, that emptiness inside, it's made me who I am."

The healing power of meditation lies in the awareness that we can no longer avoid ourselves. When we meditate, we sit with who we are. Whatever is going on is there to be seen, but as we are witnessing and not engaging it, so we can be free of any accompanying emotional turmoil. This creates the opportunity for a deeper healing.

"There's a world of difference between being lost in deeply conditioned patterns and not identifying with them," says meditation teacher **Joseph Goldstein.** "Greed arises, anger arises, fear arises, and we can become lost in that energy and then act it out. This is the cause of so much pain. Meditation is the middle ground between repression and expression, where awareness is open to the emotion, to the feeling; it is complete honesty."

One of the greatest gifts meditation gives us is the realization that nothing stays the same, not even emotions we don't particularly like, or ones that seem so enormous, important, or overwhelming. When we can sit back from anger or fear and take a breath before the emotion takes over, we can then watch it pass, often as quickly as it came. Given time, what seems vital to us now will soon lose its urgency.

When we witness without attachment, we bring awareness to selfishness, greed, anger, fear, shame or pain. Only when we cling to suffering does it stay and create more suffering. Knowing this, we can sit with whatever pain may be present, letting it in and letting it be.

> "Here it is: 'I am full of anger in this moment, I can feel it boiling in my gut, my skin is getting hot, and I want to strangle this person.' But in five minutes, that reality will change, so I needn't mistake this state for who I really am," says inspirational teacher **Joan Borysenko**.
>
> "Rather, I can accept that there are going to be times when I get angry and even that I may lose myself in that anger, especially if I resist it, but I can still accept: here it is."

Meditation also takes us beyond our limitations, allowing us to see the bigger picture of which we are just a part. No longer is our story the most important issue, nor is suffering something that only we know. The shadow has less power, it doesn't determine our behavior or run our lives.

There is a beautiful sense of rhythm that informs us that if we wait long enough even the darkest of times will pass; only when we hold on to suffering does it stay and create more suffering. Knowing this, we can sit with whatever pain may be present, letting it in and letting it be.

"At forty-three, after ten years of deep depression and despair, my real life began," says **Byron Katie**, founder of *The Work*. "I discovered that my suffering was a result of arguing with reality. I discovered that when I believed my thoughts I suffered, but that when I didn't believe them I didn't suffer. Freedom is as simple as that: suffering is optional."

4 We Are Not Alone Here: Relationship

Love Works

Every one of us, both directly and indirectly, affect each other. Everyone and everything is dependent on everything else, there is no defining place where we each begin or end.

Yet relationship creates such untold problems! Sitting in solitary bliss with our heart wide open and love pouring out toward all beings is relatively easy, but as soon as we come into direct contact with another person then all our good intentions are thrown out of the window. Our ability to stay open and loving, our selflessness and generosity, all this and more are immediately confronted by someone else's wants, needs and neuroses.

So relationship is not just an integral part of being alive, it is also the most vital and challenging teacher that any of us could ever have.

Ed comes from the Bronx and is the son of a postal worker; Deb comes from the English countryside and is of distant royal descent. As they say in England, we go together like chalk and cheese, meaning we couldn't be more different if we tried.

After 30 years of living and working together we have been there, done that, and collected a whole range of tee shirts!

And we have found that relationship is not just based on how much we love each other, but on how much we are willing to live with each other's neurosis. Here are a few guidelines that define a living relationship to us:

1. **Not to wobble at the same time**. If one of us is getting wobbly, having a challenging moment, or is in need of being heard, then the other one puts their own stuff aside and is there, present, listening.

2. **No should, should not, ought to, or ought not**. This one came into play as we began to uncover many of the assumptions, role-playing, and conditioning that we both brought to our relationship. It allowed us the freedom to be who we are, to be accepted for we are, and to be loved as we are.

3. **Meditate.** This has undoubtedly been the thread that has woven us together. Meditation reveals the endless well that constantly inspires and restores; it enables our relationship to not only survive the hard times but even to thrive. We are quite sure that by now, without meditating together, we would have retreated to opposite sides of the planet!

Meditation is an essential ingredient in a shared journey, not just because it allows us to be on the same wavelength together, but also because it creates the spaciousness to accept any differences, without the illusion of wanting things to be different. In shared silence, power struggles or one-upmanship dissolves, there is a dropping away of the superfluous, and of separation.

"Meditation enables me to practice the non-judgmental attitude I try to live by in my relationships, not only with myself and my loved ones, with clients or people in relief camps, but with my mailman and with the woman at the grocery store and with the next person I look at when I pull up to a red light," says educator **William Spear.**

Love doesn't just fall from the sky, perfect and intact. It has to be reaffirmed, remembered and renewed in every moment. But relationship could not happen if love was not already an integral part of our being. We don't need to go in search of love or pray for it to be shown to us, we have no need to protect it, no fear of losing it, or of giving away so much that we have none left. How can we lose what we truly are? How can we be left with nothing when love is the source of all life? We can never lose love; only lose sight of it.

"The Indian government invited Ed and I to speak at a yoga conference in Pondicherry, southern India," recalls **Deb**. "It was held in a huge marquee with room for a few thousand people. When it was Ed's turn to speak he talked about the beauty and awesome power of love. Then a man in the audience raised his hand.

" 'Please sir,' he said. 'What is this love that you speak of? Where can I find it? Please tell me how do I get this love?'

"Ed replied, 'You awake in love, you bathe in love, you eat in love, and you walk in love. Love is within you, it is your nature, it is who you really are.'

" 'Oh sir,' the man said. 'You have all the right answers!' "

Loving Ourselves

One of the most important aspects of meditation is getting to know ourselves (although that makes it sound as if there are two of us, when there's obviously just one, but with so many different facets), as the relationship with ourselves is the foundation for all our other relationships.

Yet we are beset with self-doubt: If I say the wrong thing will people laugh at me? How can anyone like me? Why can't I do anything right? We dislike and constantly find fault with ourselves, we think we think we are unlovable, unattractive, that we have done unacceptable things, or that we have to prove ourselves before we can be loved.

The Dalai Lama met with a group of western psychotherapists and he asked them what was the most prevalent issue that they encountered in their work. They unanimously replied that it was low self-esteem. This is the belief that says we don't deserve to be well or to be happy, that we don't believe we are good enough—a sort of built-in self-destruction clause.

It seems absurd that we should so dislike the one person we spend our life with. We have the opportunity for the most sustaining love affair of all and instead we criticize and invalidate, dismissing our needs as unimportant.

"People have a place that they think is unlovable, that something about them is unlovable," says psychologist **Gay Hendricks**. "We need to bring that unlovableness into meditation, rather than keeping it separate, rather than thinking that once we've meditated for however long then we'll get to be lovable. If we can be with our unlovableness *right now,* then it will shift. If we learn to love ourselves, then our interactions with everyone else will be different."

One of the main obstacles to believing that we are lovable just as we are is that many of us were raised to think of ourselves as fundamentally and intrinsically bad, which can lead to a deep level of inner shame. For example, Ed was often told he would never amount to anything. Such shame is corrosive; it eats away at our sense of worthiness, our self-confidence, and our ability to give or receive love.

"Even when I wasn't bad, I felt bad. And for so many years I thought that it was just me. Then I found out that 90 percent of the world feels bad at something, or they were bad at some time," says author **Debbie Ford**. "Meditation holds us with all the ways we try to get love, keep love, get approval, or try to belong. Every day we can invite ourselves to rise above the insanity of our human nature."

We may have been told that it is very self-centered, immodest, or even selfish to love ourselves, yet how can we truly love someone else if we don't? Loving ourselves is exactly where we have to start so that we can be in an honest relationship. It means being tender and gentle when we fail, picking ourselves up each time we fall, and being kind when mistakes are made. It means no more self-judgment, so that we can be ourselves without embarrassment.

As we make friends with who we are then we get to feel comfortable in our own skin. We spend our whole lives living with ourselves; it is our longest, most intimate, and most important relationship of all.

Intimacy: Into Me You See

An intimate relationship involves letting go of our defenses so another can see us for who we are, complete with all of our vulnerabilities. Which can be terrifying!

Recently, we were advising a couple experiencing problems. Tim continually gave irrelevant and meaningless reasons why he felt the relationship wasn't working, without realizing he was really expressing his own fear of letting someone see his hidden places.

Intimacy means *into me you see* but, as much as we may want to share, being seen reaches deep into our self-doubt, mistrust, and sense of inadequacy. Rather than exploring the longed-for togetherness, intimacy can make us feel exposed, emotionally naked with nowhere to hide, we retreat back into our separate corners, and are hesitant to reach out again.

> "We define ourselves as separate beings, and to stay separate we have to put a wall up around us," says musician **Krishna Das**. "We have to protect ourselves and our feelings so that no one else can see them. But this wall doesn't just protect us, it also locks us out of our hearts, and so we continue to be isolated and to suffer."

One of the great benefits of a loving relationship is it provides a safe space for all our fears—especially the ones that have never before seen the light of day—to be known and held. Love brings up everything that isn't love in order to be healed.

This is especially true as a relationship goes beyond the honeymoon phase and enters into a deepening familiarity. But it also means that, in the midst of all the good stuff, past hurt or insecurity may emerge, straining a relationship, or creating confusion and discord.

Moments like this are opportunities to breathe into the fearful places so we can come defenseless into relationship. This doesn't mean we have to be perfect before we step into intimacy—the monsters don't just pack up and move out overnight—but that we are open and willing to share.

> "Ed and I thought that we had nothing to hide from each other, but as trust grew it exposed all these places where we hadn't looked," recalls **Deb**.
>
> "My father had a big temper and lost it very easily, so I unconsciously put my own anger on hold. My first marriage ended due to the sight of my own anger. It freaked me out and that was it, I was gone.
>
> "When I married Ed, I discovered that I had a whole storeroom of anger locked away inside, but now I was able to face it. Ed was willing to receive it. I could release it without recrimination."
>
> "My mother died when I was five days old, so growing up without her I always felt no one really knew me," recalls **Ed**. "I learned how to cover it up by being an extravert; I became the most popular at school by winning all the dance contests. I even became a monk in order to protect myself from letting anyone get too close. All that to hide how fearful of intimacy I was!
>
> "As Deb and I became closer there were many moments when I felt exposed, as if I were the least lovable person in the world. That someone I loved could love me back was mind blowing!"

Intimacy isn't something that can be pulled out of a hat; it comes through meeting and knowing ourselves, and through softening and opening to each other. Instead of trying to make discomfort go away, intimacy asks that we be with the embarrassment, the shame, or the guilt, and that we gently embrace whatever we find.

"Deb and I are often asked what one thing we believe has made our marriage last as long as it has (30 years!), despite numerous ups and downs," recalls **Ed**. "It is something we both agree on: that without being able to share our feelings we remain in a separate world from each other."

Deep intimacy thrives on genuine communication. How truthful we are, how much we are able to share, how much we hold back, how we express our feelings, how well we hear and receive our partner's feelings, what we think someone else is feeling, what he or she thinks we are feeling, what we think has been said or what was not said, all this and more adds up to the need to communicate honestly and openly.

Without it then hidden resentments, secret feelings, and the 'I am right but they are wrong' syndrome grows and intimacy suffers. A lack of communication will act like a quagmire, pulling the relationship down.

"A man at one of our workshops said, 'I realize I have never really listened to people before; I was just watching their mouths move until it was my turn to speak," says psychologist **Gay Hendricks**. "We need to learn how to communicate with each other, to be able to say 'I feel hurt' or 'I feel angry' or 'I feel scared right now,' and how to really hear that without criticizing, shaming or blaming."

A lack of communication gives rise to judgment, which keeps us locked into an unending dialogue of who said what to whom, of what someone did or didn't do, of anyone or anything we disagree with. Judgment is the ego's defense: by pointing out someone else's weaknesses we think it makes us look right in comparison. But every time we judge or find fault with another we are reinforcing a sense of separateness and isolation, allowing the ego to create a gap between us.

Intimacy is giving and receiving, sharing and listening, without hidden agendas or preconceived ideas. Listening is without the desire to fix someone, to make them better, or without comparing their story to our own.

Intimacy also implies getting to know ourselves more deeply—*into me I see*. It suggests that the more we know ourselves the less need there is to hold back or have secrets, we can be open and accepting of our faults. This enables us to be much closer to someone else. When we make friends with ourselves we can make friends with others.

Which brings us to meditation and intimacy. If we meditate alone, then we experience a greater intimacy with ourselves; we can drop the preconceived story and just be as we are. When we meditate with another, then we have the possibility to come into a greater intimacy together; we meet in a deeper place, beneath the ego games, where we can connect with who we really are.

Knocking Heads

Shortly after we were married we went to India and were fortunate enough to have a private meeting with the Dalai Lama, winner of the Nobel Peace Prize, and probably the world's most famous meditator.

> "After some thirty minutes of talking together I was feeling so moved by this gentle, simple, and loving man that I just wanted to stay there," **Ed** recalls. "I really didn't want to leave! I was completely in love with this delightful being. Finally, I said to him, 'I don't want to leave, I just want to stay here with you!' I thought he would say, 'Yes, how wonderful, I see your sincerity,' but instead he just smiled and said, 'If we were together all the time, we would quarrel!'"

So relax, if the Dalai Lama can quarrel—someone who meditates for a good few hours every day—then so can we. Meditation may enable us to accept ourselves more deeply, but it doesn't stop us from having very human traits. Inevitably, there are going to be times when a relationship gets bumpy, when differences collide and egos clash, when stories and histories intrude, or needs go unmet.

When such misunderstandings or difficulties arise, we easily mistake our partner for the enemy. This can be due to our own longing to be loved; what we often want to say is "I need love," but it is far easier to think the other person is wrong than to admit that we might have needs. We cling to difficulties and make them more than they really are, replaying the irritation in our minds until we become even more upset. The ego does not want to let go!

Often a disagreement is about seeing the same thing in two different ways: one sees a white ceiling, the other sees a flat ceiling, but it's the same ceiling. If the ego is wounded in battle, then we may point the finger and see the other as the cause of our suffering, but we fail to recognize how, by holding onto hurt feelings, we are simply creating more grief for ourselves.

In India we were at an ashram, practicing yoga and meditation each day. This must sound idyllic, but we were newly married, staying in one room, and issues were accumulating.

> "On one occasion, we were having a big disagreement (we have no idea what it was about—do we ever remember the cause?) when one of the teachers walked past and overheard us," recalls **Ed**. "From outside our room, he called out to us, 'So how's the weather?' As we saw our battling egos through his eyes it reduced us to peels of laughter."

When a relationship is at its height, the two separate partners merge into each other and become one. This works wonderfully while there is concord and rapport, but as soon as there is discord, when doubt, selfishness, shame or blame arises, then we withdraw back into our separate selves, communication at a standstill. At these times of difficulty, our respective egos start to attack each other and knock heads, all in an attempt to find that place of merging again.

If we can step back from the heat of conflict and explore why someone makes us feel a certain way, it quickly becomes clear that it has very little to do with the other person and much more to do with our own reactions. Healing comes by responding to the much deeper desire for unity.

> "We had a marriage blessing at Samye Ling, a Tibetan monastery in Scotland," recalls **Deb**. "Afterwards, we asked the abbot, Akong Rinpoche, what advice he had for people in relationship.

"Akong suggested that when two people disagree (which they will) then they should both take time out by themselves to be alone, and to consider what they had done that might have contributed to the situation.

"So, rather than complaining about what someone has done to us, we look at our own behavior and the effect it is having on the other. This advice has served us well on many an occasion!"

In the quiet of meditation we can explore our attitudes, motives, or hidden agendas, and how these might be affecting our partner. How am I treating this person? What am I doing to this person to make them behave like this? Are my own dark corners influencing my behavior? How can I treat this person more kindly?

Many negative emotions arise from the emphasis we place on success and achievement, which is a left-brain activity. During meditation, we engage the right side of the brain, which encourages us to communicate in a more positive and caring way.

"It's like there may be storms on the surface of the ocean but if we drop down ten or fifteen feet, as we do in meditation, then there's no storm going on, it's calm there," says psychologist **Gay Hendricks**. "When we come back to the surface we can see that maybe nothing is really such a big deal."

In actuality, those people we have a difficult time with are really our teachers, for without an adversary, or those who trigger such strong reactions as irritation or anger, then we wouldn't have the stimulus to develop loving kindness and compassion. So we should be grateful to them for teaching us acceptance and tolerance; we can truly thank our exasperating partners, relatives, friends or colleagues for the chance to practice kindheartedness and composure!

There Is No Other

If we have no peace, it is because we have forgotten we belong to each other. Mother Theresa

In the Eastern tradition is the description of a huge net reaching in all directions with a multifaceted mirror-like jewel at each of the many knots, each jewel reflecting all the others. It is called the Jeweled Net of Indra, and it represents interconnectedness: see one and you see all within it. Not a single jewel can be separated from or is independent of any other; take just one jewel away and the net becomes unusable.

This net symbolizes how we are all interrelated and interdependent, not separate from each other any more than we are from the elephants, owls, our neighbors, the people in South Africa, or a tiger in India.

"We mistreat one another because we think of ourselves as separate beings, and feeling separated from others gives rise to fear, confusion, self-protection, grasping, anger, and aggression," says meditation teacher **Jack Kornfield**. "These states are all born out of forgetting our interdependence."

When we hold the view that "I can hurt you without hurting myself," it not only isolates us from each other but also from our connectedness, which is fundamental to our happiness. As we meditate, the more we become aware of this deep relationship.

"We are not isolated entities; we do affect each other," says meditation teacher **Ajahn Sumedho.** "If I feel a sense of 'me' as a self-centered isolated being, then I will just think of my own immediate pleasure or needs and I have no relationship or sensitivity to anything else. But as I open to the truth of our connectedness, then I have a respect for all life; I no longer see others as just there for my own selfish exploitation."

When we only see disconnection then we will continue to destruct, unaware that we are doing harm. While we were in southern Egypt, we traveled by truck into the desert. From where the truck left us, we hiked far up a dry riverbed into silence and beauty and rubbish: piles of polystyrene and plastic dumped in the middle of nowhere. In the exotic paradise of Sri Lanka, Deb was happily swimming in the beautiful Unawatuna Bay when human feces floated past her. In Thailand, we watched as villagers buried their waste in the sand, and we watched as the tide came in and dislodged the sand.

But when we see connection then healing is possible.

"Imagine that each of my two hands has the idea that it is not connected to anything else," says Zen Roshi **Bernie Glassman**. "Left hand calls itself Sally and right hand is Harry. When Sally gets cut, Harry thinks, 'I can't do anything about Sally being cut, I'm not a doctor, and I don't have a first-aid kit. And anyway, I don't want to get my new clothes stained.'

"So Harry turns away and Sally bleeds to death. But that means Harry also bleeds to death, as Harry and Sally are very attached to each other through Bernie.

"Now imagine Sally and Harry, while recognizing the separateness of each other, also recognize their oneness with Bernie. When Sally gets cut, Harry does all he can to help her because he knows that to help her is also helping both himself and Bernie.

"This is not a thinking process; it is the direct experience of the oneness of life. The appreciation of this is huge. Once we take care of the delusion of separateness, then everything else is taken care of."

Meditation enables us to end the war within ourselves. This is when we see that everything we have ever disregarded, disrespected or been frightened of is actually a part of us, that our doubt or fear is simply a reflection of our separation, from both ourselves and each other. Relationship is everywhere, in every moment.

"There are sixty of us in the meditation hall, sitting silently," says actress **Jane Fonda**. "I realize that we are all the same, as is the cat screeching in the backyard, the bird chirping, and the shiny black floor. I experience everything ultimately as one, that there is no separation. Meditation connects me to this great inwardness and unity, and at the same time there is also a great expansion into everything."

5 The Open Heart: Loving Kindness, Compassion and Forgiveness

A Deeper Happiness

"Mindfulness cultivates access to core aspects that our very sanity depends on," says mindfulness teacher **Jon Kabat-Zinn**. "It restores dimensions of our being.

"These dimensions have never actually been missing, just that we have been missing them, we have been absorbed elsewhere. When our mind clarifies and opens, our heart does the same thing."

When kindness, compassion and forgiveness are the focus of our meditation, then the changes we experience are both subtle and transformative. There is a greater ability to simply be present and available, open to the shared human condition, while embracing all as a apart of oneself.

In 1986 we first met with the Dalai Lama, at his residence in McCleod Ganj, in northern India.

"We were waiting for our meeting in a room that led off a veranda at the Dalai Lama's residence in northern India. It was a large bungalow beyond which rose the Himalayas resplendent in the morning sunshine," recalls **Deb**. "Ed wandered outside to enjoy the view.

"At that moment, he saw a monk further along the veranda beckoning for us to come. We presumed he would bring us to our meeting, but as we came closer we realized that the beckoning monk *was* the Dalai Lama.

"We immediately began to prostrate, as this is the respected way to greet a revered teacher. But the Dalai Lama took our hands and made us stand, saying, 'No, no. We are all equal here.' At first, I thought, Oh sure! You are the great Dalai Lama, spiritual leader to millions, and I am just a student. How could we possibly be equal?

"But over the following months, I felt his words in the core of my being and experienced the true equality he was referring to: the equality of our shared humanness and our shared heart."

Qualities such as loving kindness, compassion and forgiveness are like the blossoms on a tree, the flowers that transform into sweet fruits. But the self-centered ego's need for grasping, gaining, and selfishness easily buries them. We are all capable of losing our cool, getting caught up in hot emotions and causing harm. These are the weeds we need to pull up, as are moments of closed-heartedness or anger, self-doubt and insecurity. We can bring mercy and tenderness to those places, to the wounded parts, so the fight within us can come to an end. And when we step beyond ourselves, then we have the capacity to open our heart even further

"I believe the most important fruit of meditation is the opening of our hearts," says publisher **Tami Simon**. "If meditation is working, that is what it is doing. Almost every control habit I had in my life and every contraction in my body was a defense against opening my heart. But I discovered that I don't have to defend myself, I could open and be okay, that it's not going to destroy me to feel openness."

In the old Tibetan teachings, it is said that we do not really become a full human being until our heart is open and we embrace all others. Before then, we are like human animals, concerned only with our survival and uninterested in the survival of anyone else. And although our own survival is obviously important, as we move further away from the ego's self-involved version of reality we move into a place of inclusive loving kindness and compassion.

"If we take any being, whether it is our mother or father, a bug or a politician, and we put them outside of our heart, then we distort our own energy," says yoga teacher **Richard Freeman.** "We might get a little tension in the jaw or a slightly shallow breath.

"We can put others out of our life, certainly, but not out of our heart, as this leaves us disconnected. No matter how much we huff and puff or twist and turn or sit and stare, until that being is back in our heart we are essentially wasting our time. Once they are back, we immediately feel a connection with all beings. And we need to have all sentient beings in our heart as we are all connected to each one."

Loving others is actually the most self-interested thing we could do, for we gain far more from loving and caring and helping than we do from self-centeredness. It gives us an unmatched joy in being. When the open arms of love replace the closed arms of fear, then delight and happiness replace dread and isolation.

"When we discover inner happiness, it wells up out of our being," says Professor **Robert Thurman**. "We realize this through the deepening of awareness, that thinking of others is really much more selfish and fulfilling than thinking of ourselves.

"When we get out of the little self and embrace others as ourselves then we focus on their happiness, which means we have a much bigger pool of happiness."

Embracing Loving Kindness

The story goes that, at the time of the Buddha, a group of monks wanted to do a quiet meditation retreat, away from the crowds of followers. So the Buddha told them about a lovely glade in the forest where they could go. He promised they would be undisturbed.

The monks found their way to the glade and settled down to meditate. But what they didn't know was that the glade was inhabited by a gang of tree spirits who were highly upset that these monks should come and make themselves so at home in their glade.

When tree spirits want to they can be extremely scary, ugly, very smelly, and unbelievably noisy, ferociously shrieking all over the place. They did everything they could to spook the hermits and make them leave. And it worked. As there was no peace, the monks could not possibly meditate, so they hurried back to the Buddha and begged him to let them go somewhere else.

But no. Instead, the Buddha taught them a meditation practice of loving kindness, or *metta* in Sanskrit, which develops loving kindness toward all beings, including our adversaries and ourselves. Then he sent the monks back to the forest. His famous last words were, "This is the only protection you will need."

Despite thinking the Buddha must be mad, nevertheless the monks reluctantly returned to the glade, sat down and began practicing what they had been taught. And it worked! The tree spirits, which at first were very displeased to see the monks come back, no longer had any effect on them. For all their antics, the meditators just kept sitting there.

Long story short, eventually the tree spirits were won over by the waves of loving kindness emanating from the robed ones and, far from chasing them away, the same nasties that had been so ferocious now became disciples.

The question is, who are the tree spirits? It seems they are everything that goes on in our minds that keeps distracting us: all the doubts, insecurities, fears, anger, the list goes on. And the point is that loving kindness has the ability to transform all manner of monsters and ghouls, proving how meditation enables us to overcome any obstacles, and that love is way more powerful than any opposing force.

Rather than trying to eliminate negativity, we cultivate the opposite; seeing and knowing pain, we bring kindness. Doesn't this sound wonderful? That all we have to do is be kind and loving? How great, what a cool idea!

But in practice it's not always so easy, such as when someone says or does something that is hurtful. Can kindness still emanate when the ego is upset? Can love still flow when the heart has withdrawn? Through loving kindness meditation we get to see all those places that are bound in selfishness and greed.

"I had an interview with a meditation teacher, and I said, 'All I really know is to try to be kind,'" says author **Marc Ian Barasch**.

"And he said, 'I think you've got it!' And I thought, great, I got the gold star.

"But then he said, 'And now you have to get used to it!' Meaning, it's fine to have this understanding, but how does it saturate my life? How can I remember to be kind and have empathy for someone, even if they're mad at me, they're thwarting me, or they're in my way? We have to create a gap between action and reaction, and that's what meditation allows us to do."

Loving kindness meditation starts with directing this quality toward ourselves. How much easier it would be if we could just skip this bit and start straight in with loving others! But without a true caring and kindness for ourselves then our capacity to direct friendship toward anyone else is limited, it can't be genuine or unconditional.

Bringing loving kindness into our lives means every time we say something uncalled for, make a fool of ourselves, or feel unworthy, instead we bring gentleness, acceptance, and friendship.

"Be caring and compassionate to yourself," says author **Debbie Ford**. "Ninety-nine percent of the abuse that happens is going on inside ourselves. If we want a change, then that's where we have to start. As I learn this myself, I get softer and kinder with who I am. Each one of us can be kinder to ourselves."

We keep inviting kindness into any self-negation or lack of self-esteem. This is not about brushing over places where we need to take responsibility for our behavior, but about embracing the humanness within us that caused such behavior to begin with.

In times of stillness we create a space where self-doubt, fear, mistrust, or any other emotion can come, be seen and known. For how can an open heart discriminate or turn away from itself?

"By developing a sense of respect for others and a concern for their welfare," says the **Dalai Lama**, "we reduce our own selfishness, which is the source of all problems, and enhance our sense of kindness, which is a natural source of goodness."

Loving kindness, or *metta,* means both gentle and friend, that we can be a kind and gentle friend to both others and ourselves. It is like soft rain falling on dry earth. This quality of friendliness does not pick and choose; for loving kindness to be authentic it is through being a friend to all.

We watched as an eager young CNN news reporter asked the Dalai Lama what was the first thing he thought of when he awoke in the morning. We thought that this most revered leader would say something deeply profound or insightful along the lines of vowing to save the world from its own ignorance. Instead, he simply replied, "Shaping my motivation." He then added that shaping his motivation on a daily basis constantly reminds him to extend loving kindness to all beings.

Which made us realize that every step of the way we are challenged to live with honesty, integrity and care. Motivation guides our behavior and determines whether our intent is arising out of selfishness or selflessness. Is our motivation one of kindness, or is it one of judgment? Are we making someone else seem wrong in order for us to appear right? Or are we genuinely feeling consideration, respect, and care?

"Meditation without vision would be absolutely empty, while action without the knowledge, wisdom, passion, and love gained from meditation is useless," says author **Andrew Harvey**. "We need the clarity of meditation to awake and guide our motivation."

Releasing Negativity

> "Some years ago, we were attending a wedding at Karma Dzong, a Tibetan center in Boulder, Colorado," recalls **Deb**. "Chögyam Trungpa, who was conducting the marriage ceremony, said to the aspiring couple, 'If you can make friends with one person, then you can make friends with the world.'"

It is relatively effortless to extend loving kindness outward, like the ripples on a pond, from ourselves toward our family, friends and loved ones. But for loving kindness to be genuine it can't just end with the people we already know and love.

The ripples have to go further, outward toward those we don't know and those we may not like, and even those we are having a hard time with, where negative issues have arisen that are pulling the relationship apart, or where there is anger, resentment and dislike.

We constantly cause suffering: we hurt ourselves, we hurt each other, ignore each other's pain and create further pain. How do we stay open and loving in the midst of insult or conflict? When we are affected by someone being dismissive, hurtful or hostile, then it's like there is a hook in us for that negativity to grab hold of, a place where it can land that triggers all our hidden feelings of unworthiness, insecurity, doubt, or self-dislike.

However, when we extend loving kindness toward such a person, as we can in meditation, an extraordinary thing happens: the landing place, or the hook within, begins to dissolve. There is nowhere for the negativity to take hold.

"I was the administrator for an educational institute in Hawaii, and for some reason the main teacher really had it in for me," recalls **Deb**. "No matter what I did, she disagreed or made me wrong. I realized she was triggering childhood issues of being ignored or disregarded, as I would shrink into a small, ineffective place when I was around her.

"It then emerged that I was going to have to go with her and the class (who had also been turned against me) to a remote cabin for a one-week wilderness program. The only option I had was to focus on her during my loving kindness meditation practice, which I did every day for a few weeks before we left and continued while we were there.

"By the time we got to the cabin her attitude had begun to subtly change: she was no longer making me the cause of everything that went wrong. Over the next few days she changed even more, slowly acknowledging me, and by the end of the week she was actually including me, once even asking for my opinion.

"It was amazing to see that she didn't notice anything was unusual or different. All I had done was practice loving kindness meditation, through which the hook that she had been hanging all her judgment on had dissolved within me. She had nowhere to put her negativity so it fell on the floor between us. Eventually it just slunk away, unable to find a home."

As we bring loving kindness to the adversary, all manner of feelings may arise about what happened, who said what to whom, or what someone did or didn't do. We can accept those feelings, while also letting go of the story. Who did or said what is not relevant; what matters is the shared human experience. Hurt, disagreement and anger arise when we forget our essential unity and hang out in separate, isolated places. By releasing the story, we are able to go beyond the ego's affront.

The negative reactions that arise during moments of discord or disagreement can cause continued suffering and inner conflict. Extending kindness toward the adversary is, therefore, really extending it toward ourselves. It frees the pain, which enables us to find our balance.

Then the ripples can go further, now toward all beings, whoever and wherever they are. This can highlight hidden issues of prejudice and resistance. Can we really extend loving kindness toward terrorists, rapists or dictators as easily as we can toward caregivers, charity workers, or our loved ones? Can we find a place in our heart where all beings are equal?

Prejudice goes very deep. It is only healed when we accept those parts of ourselves we find unacceptable. Then we have the courage to include those who are dissimilar to us, who have different beliefs, are a different color, or who live a different lifestyle. When we can tolerate ourselves then we can be tolerant of others others and extend kindness to all.

Many of the people we spoke with for this book had a personal history of emotional dysfunction, drug abuse, illness, or depression, some were suicidal or spent time in jail. When such a background is used as fuel for personal transformation then the inner torment becomes the impetus for both meaningful change and for opening the heart.

Mahatma Gandhi famously said, "You must be the change you want to see in the world." In other words, if we want to have more love in our lives, we need to become more loving; if we genuinely want to help bring peace to the world, then we must start by ending the war within.

Awakening Compassion

"In all of the Asian languages, the word for mind and the word for heart is the same word. If you see the mind and heart are the same, then compassion is built right into it," says mindfulness teacher **Jon Kabat-Zinn**. "Mindful attention is itself affectionate. It's open, spacious, curious, and in the seeing of the interconnectedness, then compassion arises naturally as there is no separation."

Loving kindness and compassion are such clear outcomes of meditation that they are now scientifically verifiable. There is an overwhelming amount of research showing how meditation charges the circuits in the part of the brain associated with contentment and happiness, while measured brain wave patterns indicate the positive effects of sitting quietly. Buddhist monks, with many hours of meditation practice, have had their minds systematically studied; when asked to focus on compassion, their brains reflected an intensified activity.

Few of us are able to meditate as much as a Buddhist monk, but data also shows that meditating for as little as five minutes each day can produce discernable changes in the brain in a matter of just a few weeks. This means that we can purposefully develop qualities such as loving kindness and compassion within ourselves.

"There are tremendous possibilities for radical transformation, and meditation can make a dramatic difference to destructive emotions," says professor **Richard Davidson.** "The effect of meditation on the circuitry in the brain clearly shows a real change in a way that can transform anger and fear. Meditation practices designed to cultivate kindness and compassion alter the brain in many positive ways."

We have a newspaper photograph of Bishop Tutu, with his hands held in prayer position. Beneath it are his words, *Please make it fashionable to be compassionate.* That photograph is many years old, but his words are even more relevant today.

We have already proven that war does not work, that fighting and killing in the name of religion, to gain domination, or to claim control, never has a happy ending. Generosity, loving kindness and compassion are really the only choices we have yet to try.

Heart-centered qualities such as these are innate within; they can't be bought from a store or obtained from somewhere outside. There is a tender quality in each one of us that is loving and caring. Without such tenderness then kindness would not be possible, compassion would not be possible.

"Take care of the person next to you," says Zen Roshi **Bernie Glassman**. "It might be your spouse, your child, your parents, or it might be a stranger. It doesn't matter who it is and it doesn't matter if they have nothing to give you; you just do it because it's there to be done."

There will be times when we hurt each other, when we ignore each other's needs; there will be moments of insult or conflict. As we open the heart and develop compassion we pay attention to such times, we can witness the suffering we see around us without turning away from it or pretending it isn't there: the victims of abuse, senseless fighting, the homeless, or selfishness and greed. Rather than getting caught in the details we have a more inclusive awareness.

"How do we go from the discovery that we are basically trapped in this ego state to universal compassion?" says author **Marc Ian Barasch**. "There's a natural tendency to look after ourselves first, to react against things that seem to threaten us. To get from that sort of automatic response to compassion takes something extra, and that extra is meditation.

"Meditation moves us from the insatiable feeling that we are the ego to a broader understanding that maybe the ego is not as solid or important as we think it is. It's a deliberate shift from awareness of self to awareness of others."

Compassion is seeing the aggression and intolerance within ourselves: the anger, irritation, fear and insecurity. By bringing tenderness to these wounded parts, the war inside can stop. Compassion is our ability to be with another's pain and suffering, but we can only do this when we have brought kindness to our own pain.

"Love and compassion are necessities, not luxuries. Without them, humanity can't survive," says Zen Roshi **Joan Halifax**.

"What happens through meditation is the growing sense of friendship with the whole world. This includes trees, rivers, mountains, animals. We spontaneously and innately feel loving kindness, compassion and deep friendship toward all beings and all things."

Alongside compassion, we also need to see with awareness and discernment. This is known as *wise compassion*, action that is inherently skillful and aims to bring release from suffering; its opposite is known as *idiot compassion,* which doesn't see the whole situation and so, although it looks compassionate, it can actually increase suffering. For instance, offering candy to a starving child is misguided kindness because they need food, not sugar. Idiot compassion is also seen when we support or

condone another's neurosis. The balance of these two qualities—compassion and wise discernment—is essential for us to
know where pity is masquerading as kindness.

In other words, compassion is both the embrace of suffering, and the ability to not support ignorance. This means
seeing a situation and the cause of the suffering clearly so that
pain can be resolved and further suffering avoided. As such,
compassion is universally essential.

"In a monastery, in the highlands of central Tibet, we
had the opportunity for an audience with the abbot,"
says author **Gregg Braden**. "I asked him, 'In your experience, in your teachings, and in your world view, what
is the stuff that holds the universe together? What is it
that connects us all?'

"The translator and the abbot had a banter going
back and forth about how to answer this question.
Finally, the translator turned to me and he said just
one word. That was his answer, one word. I thought it
was a mistranslation, that I had heard him wrong, so
I asked again. And he came back with the same word.

"He said that the force that holds the stuff in the
universe together is compassion.

" 'Wait a minute,' I said. 'Are you telling me that compassion is a force of nature that exists everywhere in the
universe, or are you telling me that it is an experience
that we create in our bodies?'

"The abbot and the translator went back and forth
again, and then the translator just said, 'Yes.'

"He was telling me that we have the capability to
create within our own being the very experience that
aligns and attunes us with our world, because it is all
linked through this field of compassion."

Discovering Forgiveness

Without forgiveness, human society and existence are impossible.
Bishop Tutu

We attended a conference on men's issues. Brian was on stage describing the abuse that he had received from his father when he was a child. Among other things, his father had threatened him by holding a shotgun to his head. This was serious abuse, and Brian talked about it with anger and bitterness. He said quite emphatically that he would never be able to forgive his father. After Brian had spoken, there followed a few minutes of stunned silence.

Then a man at the back of the room stood up and said, "If you can't forgive then you can't dance."

What was so eloquently voiced in those few words describes exactly the emotional holding that takes place when there is no forgiveness. Our ability to dance—to move emotionally, to give, to love, to feel alive and free—gets stuck. All the pain, grief, and hurt are held in this immovable or frozen place. We can't move forward when a part of us is locked in the past, and we can't be in the present as memories from the past are constantly pulling us away.

All around us is the evidence of a lack of forgiveness: broken families, self-hate, guilt and shame leading to depression, huge amounts of fear and anger, bitterness, prejudice, self-righteousness, and closed-heartedness.

"I worked in a nursing home where I saw numerous residents clinging to incidents from their past: words said in anger, or distorted memories of how they had been wronged by children who had disagreed with them," recalls

Deb. "So much bitterness. They couldn't heal their differences with their children and come together, even now, so near to dying, as their hurt and anger had become solid and immovable, like prison bars surrounding them."

When we feel guilt and shame at our own behavior, or hurt and rage at someone else's—it makes no difference which—then the emotion from that incident can get buried inside. We learn to live by ignoring this denied, repressed place without realizing how deeply limiting it is, how it holds back our joy and happiness along with the shame or anger.

The beauty of meditation is our deepening self-awareness. We gain a greater impartiality, whether of our own behavior or that of others. We step back from the attached storyline and witness emotions just as they are. As awareness grows of our interconnectedness—that others are an integral part of us—so compassion arises, which naturally gives rise to forgiveness. It's not possible to have one without the other.

There is a hugely mistaken view that such qualities as compassion, tolerance, and especially forgiveness are expressions of weakness. Yet it takes great strength to forgive, great courage and fortitude of heart. As Bishop Tutu says, "If someone thinks that forgiveness is a sign of weakness, then they haven't tried it!"

"Forgiveness is 'giving forth' in such a way that it releases us from those things that have kept us entrained in fear, hatred, and the great illusion of separation," says visionary **Jean Houston**. "It is this illusion that we are separate that regards the other as a stranger. Forgiveness meditation releases that which has held us back from the ability to engage with all others, all creatures, in a radical sense of love."

Forgiving Ourselves

"One of the hardest stories or definitions to give up is our definition of ourselves as a victim," says spiritual teacher **Gangaji**. "We have all experienced being hurt by someone, such as our parents or a lover. But it's not about denying the hurt, it's actually about opening and meeting the hurt, and then the hurt itself becomes a deepening of our heart. In that moment, it is natural for forgiveness to occur."

We usually think that forgiveness is about forgiving someone else: this other person has done this wrong thing, and I am hurt, angry, and upset. It is the strongest position to be in, as we are the abused or victimized one and the other is the abuser who has done the dirty deed.

However, in a recent workshop, we asked how many people were carrying around a hidden secret about something they could not forgive themselves for. At least three-quarters of the participants put up their hands. We can find forgiveness very hard to give to ourselves.

We try to avoid looking inside our dark corners, but accumulated guilt, shame, or self-dislike can become familiar crutches for the ego, affecting our activities and behavior. Guilt for what we have done stays with us long after the event: I am such a bad, hopeless, useless, awful, uncaring, unlovable person who never gets it right. We even believe guilt is our atonement, that through it we are somehow redeeming our wrong doing, when in reality all it does is create more suffering.

Blame follows guilt: How could I have done such a thing? How can I ever trust myself? How can I ever be trusted by anyone else? Shame and self-dislike debilitate our joy, leaving us lonely and miserable.

When we hurt someone else it is rarely because we are feeling totally wonderful and just fancy making someone suffer for the fun of it. It is usually because somewhere deep inside there is pain. In our attempt to ignore, repress or deny that pain, we lash out and hurt whoever is there. Simple equation: what is going on inside will get expressed on the outside.

In meditation, we get to touch the pain inside us that has spilled over and caused pain to someone else. It may be that what we did was wrong, but we can forgive ourselves by accepting the ignorance, selfishness or closed heartedness that caused us to act this way. Who we were when we did what we are feeling so guilty about is not who we are now.

> "My son was nine years old when his father and I got divorced," says workshop participant **Carol Armstrong**. "I couldn't cope as a single parent, I was destroyed inside. I knew my son was suffering; he was so lonely and unhappy. So I took the monumental decision to send him away to boarding school. It felt like the very best I could do for him. But he hated it! He ran away twice! It broke my heart to send him back. He eventually adapted and was happy there.
>
> "Years later he accused me of abandoning him. I had to remember what was happening for me at the time and how I was sure I was doing the right thing for him. When I remembered, then I was able to forgive myself."

Forgiveness occurs every time we criticize or blame ourselves for being hopeless, wrong, stupid, for all the self-dislike and self-denial, for thinking that we deserve the bad things that happen or that we must have done something wrong to be so abused, for thinking we should have known better as it was all our fault, for abandoning ourselves, for ignoring or denying our own needs, and for believing that guilt or shame are somehow redeeming our wrong-doing.

The truth is we are going to cause harm and be harmed simply because we are human. But while knowing that we can't change the past, we can change our attitude toward it. Meditation gives us spaciousness from whatever we may have done, consciously or unconsciously, where we can witness what we said or did without judgment. When we practice forgiveness meditation we can see the story, let it go, and then go beyond it.

"I know that we have to forgive, but actually we need to ask for forgiveness as well. I don't know if I have helped more than I've done damage, or if I have hurt as much as I have helped," says psychotherapist **Maura Sills.**

"I ask forgiveness for all that I have done, knowingly and unknowingly, consciously or unconsciously, and in return I truly forgive you for what you may have done, knowingly or unknowingly, that has affected me and taken me away from my better good.

"We get entangled in all of this suffering and confusion. When we can ask for and give forgiveness, we walk away slightly more humble in what we do and how we are."

Forgiving Others

A Sufi holy man was asked what forgiveness is. He said, "It is the fragrance that flowers give when they are crushed."

Forgiving someone else for the harm he or she has done is not easy, as we are the ones feeling the pain, not them. But how many times have we rerun the tape, gone over the details of who said what to whom, of how it all happened, of hidden motives, of the injustice and blame, or the guilt and shame? And did this ever help us feel better, more healed or happier? How often do we have to rehash the deed before we see that it is prolonging our unhappiness?

There is a well-known story of two Auschwitz survivors walking together. One asks the other if he has forgiven Hitler. The other replies, "No, of course not, how could I forgive such atrocities?" The first one then says, "So you are still in prison."

We are not trying to be simplistic here. From a rational point of view, it can seem impossible to forgive: we are hurt; it is the other person's fault, so why should we forgive them when they are to blame? However, when someone hurts us they are not acting from a caring or loving place; their greed and selfishness, hatred or ignorance are ruling their behavior.

Forgiveness does not mean a repression of pain, nor does it mean to forget; it is not a denial of what happened, which simply puts our feelings in some distant recess from where they reemerge at a later date. Rather, to forgive includes fully acknowledging how angry, upset, abused, betrayed, or bitter we may be, how let down or sad we feel, and that it is absolutely okay to feel this way.

Without forgiveness it is like carrying around heavy baggage that weighs us down so we can't go forward with it, but we can't go without it as this bag contains our history. Or it is like walking around in very dark sunglasses that distort reality while also creating a barrier that keeps us locked away from happiness.

If we want to reach a place of healing and emotional freedom, then we have to confront the desire to hold on to the story, to keep replaying the details, or to stay resentful, for this causes us further suffering while maintaining our separation from ourselves.

We were at a talk in London where we watched Jo Berry walk on stage alongside Pat Magee, the man who had planted an IRA (Irish Republican Army) bomb that killed Jo's father, politician Sir Anthony Berry. You could have heard a pin drop as they each spoke about coming to understand the pain behind such a violent act of betrayal.

> "An inner shift is required to hear the story of the enemy," says author **Jo Berry**. "For me the question is always about whether I can let go of my need to blame, and open my heart enough to hear Patrick's story and to understand his motives. The truth is that sometimes I can and sometimes I can't. ... no matter which side of the conflict you're on, had we lived each others lives we could all have done what the other did."

We do not have to forgive the act, which may have been reprehensible, but what we can forgive is the ignorance that led to the act. This is the ignorance of our essential interconnectedness—that what I do to you I am also doing to myself. Releasing the past, the story and the details, the ignorance and the selfishness, we can open to the present, to who we are now.

The beauty of forgiveness is it removes the power that others may have over us. As long as we continue to feel hurt or angry, then the abuser still has the upper hand. In this way, forgiveness has nothing to do with anyone else; it is still effective even if the other person doesn't know. The forgiveness is for ourselves.

> "Finally, in my mid-thirties, I realized that I no longer needed my father's affirmation," recalls **Deb**. "I had touched into a deeper acceptance of myself. And, as the need was released, so I could see the confused man for who he was, someone who had no idea how to love, only to cause pain. As I separated his pain from mine, I was finally able to let go and heal."

Forgiveness is truly revolutionary. Just as an oyster uses the irritation from a grain of sand to produce the beauty of a pearl, so we can transform fear and hate into kindness and caring. Meditation deepens our awareness, enabling us to witness the other just as they are, free of our projections, hurts or fears. Forgiveness continues in every moment we are not fully present, fully open. It is a daily meditation to make friends with what we see in our own mind. By recognizing this truth, we are able to honor our shared humanness. What a gift!

6 Off the Cushion And Into The World

Meditation In Action

"My meditation practice has evolved over the years so that it's not separate from any other part of my life," says life coach **Judith Ansara**. "It's not separate from my reaching out to touch another, from getting my guests some tea, from working with a client, from being kind to someone in a grocery line.

"Meditation is the fabric of my life rather than something I do. It's the awareness of breath, of sensation, and the intention to leave a trail of beauty behind me. When I go to the grocery store, how can I leave a trail of beauty behind me? When I am working with a client, how can I do that? It's taking meditation into life so that everywhere we go we leave a trail of beauty."

We take meditation off the cushion in the way we deal with demanding children, a needy parent, or a business partner. We do it in our capacity to let go of conflicts and forgive mistakes. We do it by meeting challenging situations with presence, skillfulness, and equanimity. We do it in how we treat the physical world around us. And we do it in our desire to reach out to others, perhaps through feeding the hungry, cleaning polluted waterways, or working for political change.

This doesn't mean we have to become world movers and shakers, for awareness and kindness is just as evident in the smaller details of our lives, such as smiling or holding a door for a stranger. We are all capable of caring.

"We may think, 'I'm not beautiful, I don't have any qualities that would be useful.' What a hubris that is, to think the world has singled you out to be useless and unbeautiful!" says mindfulness teacher **Jon Kabat-Zinn**. "It is better to ask, 'What can I do that would contribute even in the tiniest way to greater levels of kindness?' Even the act of taking your seat for meditation is a radical act of love that extends way beyond your small self."

We put meditation into action when we see beyond our ego-needs to our connectedness with all beings; when reaching out beyond ourselves becomes an unaffected and spontaneous expression of who we are. This is not the same as being a martyr, or ignoring our own needs. We care for ourselves equally, but we are no longer obsessed with putting ourselves first.

"It becomes impossible to live for yourself, to live life on the 'me plan.' That is the point of meditation—to get out of the narrow confines of self," says Agape minister **Michael Bernard Beckwith**. "It becomes impossible to close your eyes to a world filled with the suffering of others. The real point is what we do when we leave our meditation cushion, our church pew, our synagogue, mosque, or temple."

In a world where self-interest is the norm, it takes great courage not to react with greed or anger, both of which can and do cause harm. Harmlessness, or *ahimsa* in Sanskrit, sounds simple but requires a deeper shift in attitude.

Ahimsa asserts that causing harm never creates peace, whether between people, countries, or within our own lives. This means that the same issues that cause indignation or even rage can instead generate compassion. And although anger may be appropriately used on occasion, compassion can be used without hesitation in every situation.

None of us get through life without causing harm. How many times a day, consciously or otherwise, do we put ourselves down, reaffirm our hopelessness, or see ourselves as incompetent and unworthy? How much resentment, guilt, or shame are we holding on to, thus harming our self-esteem and stopping us from caring and loving? How often do we ignore someone else's feelings?

What do we do when a fly gets trapped inside the window, or there's a spider in the bathtub? When we are in a good mood we'll take time to open the window and let the fly go, or to get the spider out before we have a bath. But if we are upset, angry or stressed then we won't think twice about swatting the fly or flushing the spider down the drain.

In other words, inner pain or torment will spill out and harm anyone or anything in its way.

While the Dalai Lama is known for his non-violent and compassionate beliefs, it is less known that he rises at four a.m. each day to meditate for at least two hours. Which doesn't mean we all have to do the same, but it does show the important role meditation plays in our ability to be skillful, kinder, and act with greater harmlessness.

Skillful action brings out the best in each situation and encourages generosity and kindness, while unskillful actions maintain and reinforce separation; they are basically harmful and self-centered. The opportunities for skillful behavior are present in every moment, from dealing with someone complaining to making sure your kids get an equal amount of attention, from running a business meeting to having to negotiate a peace treaty.

> "I meditate so that I can be a kinder and saner human being in the world. It keeps me out of trouble with myself or with others, and allows me to be the caring person that I really want to be," says sound therapist **Vickie Dodd**. "I have always viewed meditation as a very practical ingredient in my life; I need it in order to be a human being that can walk with sensitivity and generosity."

Moms & Meditation

We are not proud parents of delightful offspring, so we asked **Kiri Westby** to write this piece on moms and meditation. Kiri is a longtime meditator, change-maker, and the mother of two small children.

Taking A Lap

Meditation and motherhood: this may appear to be an oxymoron, as the words conjure up images that seem contradictory—the serene meditator enjoying the silence in their quiet mind, versus the frazzled, unkempt mother surrounded by chaos. But many years working in war zones taught me something new: the power of meditative moments. Short, conscious moments of calm, infused throughout the day, can be one's most useful tool against the confusion and disorder of parenting.

One morning, in the Democratic Republic of Congo, the air still ripe with the echoes of last night's bullets, I sat at the foot of my hotel room bed and practiced listening meditation. It was all I could think to do to slow my terrified, rapid heartbeat. I stilled my mind, closed my eyes, and opened my ears.

At first, I only heard the sound of military grade vehicles and sirens. Then, beneath, the wail of a baby, the beat of African drums pulsing through transistor radio static, and a woman laughing—reminders of humanity's common desire for peace, a fresh moment to connect to something bigger and more sane than war. My heart slowed, I opened to the day ahead, whatever would come.

For me, motherhood has been a bit like working in a war zone. Not to diminish what living through war is like, but the constant vigilance, the drain on the adrenal system, the sustained lack of sleep and the loss of regular bathing and meals, all felt very familiar with my firstborn. And, as such, some of the meditation practices I had adapted to my life as a human rights activist became applicable.

Here's a practice I have called: Taking a Lap:

Both kids are screaming now, because it's a cruel fact that when one child starts screeching, like Macaws, the other will inevitably chime in. In the cacophony it's hard to distinguish one's needs from the other and, to be honest, I don't really care. I've reached my edge. Every parent has one.

This is the crucial moment I take my lap.

Whether they need to be in the car or not, I strap the kids into their five-point harnesses, roll up the windows, close the car doors and exhale, knowing they are safe and immobilized. I drop into my listening mind. Taking a deep breath, I look to the sky and push all of my frustration out in one loud sigh. Then, placing my attention on my feet, I walk slowly, heel to toe, around the car. To an outsider, it may appear as though I'm simply taking the long way around to the driver's seat, but in my mind I am a wandering ascetic, and to my nervous system each step is a healing balm.

Heel to toe ... heel to toe ... I listen.

At first, I hear the sounds of other cars in the parking lot, groceries being hauled into power-lifted cargo doors. Then, underneath, a teenager crying at the coffee shop next door, her heartache palpable in each sob. And there, way in the background, the birds singing loudly while the air itself makes music through the trees, just as it always has; another fresh moment to reconnect.

No matter which shrieks come pouring through the door, whether laughter or tears, I know that it's workable. In one three-minute, conscious lap

around the car, that edge, so solid only moments before, softens. I am a
warrior newly readied for battle...

I married a man who was hit by his father for misbehaving. My own grandfather hit my dad and his brothers from pent up frustration and anger. In fact, four out of five Americans believe it is "sometimes appropriate" to spank children. Part of the problem is that violence is learned and it is cyclical: our children literally navigate the world by watching our every move, and that's a lot of pressure. Add in sleep-deprivation, financial stress, and a pace of life that could make Olympic athletes tire, and it's not hard to see how we can fall into behaviors that allow our micro-aggressions to take center stage.

My antidote lays in practicing meditative moments.

"What were you looking for mommy?" my three year old asks after watching me stare at the asphalt as I slowly crept around the car.

"My sanity," I reply.

"Oh, did you find it?" she asks, hopefully.

"Yes I did," I can honestly say. "It was somewhere between the back bumper and the rear right tire."

And this is how I've come to bridge the sacred world of meditation with the profane reality of motherhood; by carving out short moments of "big mind," I can better handle life's "small minded" moments. Instead of recreating the painful patterns of our pasts, we have the unique opportunity to spin a different tale for our grandchildren.

The other day my now six-year-old girl wandered into the forest, heel to toe ... heel to toe ... saying she was looking for "her calm." I knew then, if nothing else, that my often desperate, sometimes ridiculous-looking moments of street side walking meditation has provided her with the invisible tool my own mother gifted me decades ago, a tool that's saved me from coming unhinged time and again.

When it comes to meditation and motherhood, my only advice is to create your own meditative moments and practice them regularly, so when you come up against your edgier places you will know exactly what to do with them.

Kids & Meditation

> "I do this thing with the children where I say, 'Breathing in, I calm my body; breathing out, I smile. Breathing in, I know today is wonderful; breathing out, I know this moment is beautiful.' When I do that they all jump for joy," says entertainer **Wavy Gravy**. "It is very cool."

Teaching a child how to be still and quiet has numerous obstacles, as any mom would testify to. But children can actually be the easiest to teach, as they are free of the mental arguments against meditation that derail many adults. We may need to be creative in how we teach, but often it is the influence of a parent meditating that will encourage them most, as Jae found with her young son, Amdo, as relayed in the HuffingtonPost.com:

> "As a toddler, Amdo was fascinated by my meditation practice. So I soon gave him gentle guidance," says Jae. "I said, 'Feel what it's like to feel a tingle in your fingertips.' You have to be really still to do this.
>
> "There was one time when I was really agitated, and spontaneously Amdo said, 'Mom, feel your fingertips!'"

How or when we teach meditation to children may depend on their needs, for all children are different. But it is always good to start with just a few minutes of either breathing or visualization. If we start with breathing, then make it fun like alternative nostril breathing, belly breathing, or counting breaths from one to three. Visualization may be of each part of the body, from toes to head. Or try chanting together, whether just one word or a few.

"I taught children meditation in India, at a school based on yoga philosophy," recalls **Ed**. "It was brilliant the way they responded, especially when it was fun. I would teach them laughing meditation, and they would sit and just giggle. It relaxed them from the uptightness of being in school. They were able to be themselves without hesitation; there is no threat when love becomes the norm.

"On coming back to the US, I began teaching Mickey Mouse meditation. It was a huge success! It helped the kids to relax and to focus."

When children meditate they are less distracted and more attentive. This means they are able to process any concerns or negativity, to let go of old stuff without focusing on the story or needing to analyze it. Mindfulness frees them so their innate tendencies can come to the surface. We should all become like kids!

"Yoga makes me feel calm, and the relaxation at the end of class is like taking a nap, but better." Ryder, age eight.

Alongside the growing awareness of mindfulness and meditation is the increasing number of schools offering these to children. It varies from starting and ending each day with a few minutes of silence, to sitting in a darkened room for 15 minutes, to lying down and belly breathing. They can be instructed to focus on where they feel the breath in their nose tips, or to see a glowing bubble moving through their body.

As a result attendance levels have risen, concentration levels have risen, exam passes have risen, while bullying rates have lowered, all due to stress, anxiety, and a lack of self-esteem levels coming down. More and more schools are offering trainings in mindfulness, so as to enable a greater awareness of the present moment for all.

"Our children live with the same electronic devices as we do and are immersed in the same torrent of emotional over-stimulation," says yoga educator **Tara Guber**. "Now add the social demands of growing up, being accepted, and finding your own unique qualities and passions. How do children get the peace of mind necessary to learn and understand who they really are?

"A mere five minutes a day of mindful breathing produces immediate and lasting results, especially in school, such as: relaxation, improved focus, concentration, comprehension, and increased energy. These are all core metacognitive skills that are essential for effective learning. And best of all, the effects are cumulative: the more children develop a daily practice of mindfulness and meditation, the more the physiological, psychological and emotional benefits increase.

"By prioritizing 'Time IN,' or a few minutes of silence and reflection, children attain and maintain a true peace of mind that is the foundation for a healthy and fulfilling life."

There is also the effect of meditation on those working with children, such as teachers or therapists, and how the children may change as a result. The one who is meditating is able to stay more present and openhearted, while the child can receive and respond to that awareness. It's a kind of second-hand benefit.

"Meditation has changed everything, especially my work with children," says play therapist **Megan Cronin Larson.** "The pausing has been profound. It has invited me to arrive in the here and now with my child clients, and to accept whatever happens without labeling, judging, or categorizing behavior.

"This awareness has allowed the children to fully show up as they are, with the freedom to work on whatever they need to. By modeling my own present moment awareness, they drop in and experience the present moment for themselves. Once they recognize their own suffering, realize they are not alone with it, that they have choices in managing it, then the healing is able to take place.

"My favorite moment is when a child whispers to me, 'I just took a big breath!' because I know that through conscious breathing they can understand and be at ease with their emotional experiences. When they feel stressed or scared they can soothe themselves; when they make their exhalations longer they calm themselves; by focusing on the in and out breath they bring themselves into a state of balance. This can be a revelation as it means they are no longer victims of their emotional world."

Silence In The Boardroom

We received a phone call and the voice on the other end simply asked, "Do you teach meditation?" Ed replied that we did. The voice said, "We would like you to come to Thailand to teach our CEOs." The previous year, it had been golf; this year, the VP wanted to try meditation.

So we went to teach these highly stressed top-management bosses the simple art of being quiet. We had no idea if they had understood what we were doing but on the last day, when they were free to do whatever they wanted, such as play golf or shop, one of them requested a meditation session. To our amazement, they all showed up.

We have met with many companies that want to integrate mindfulness and meditation into their workplace. Now meditation is taught in Google, Yahoo!, Target, General Mills, and the Seahawks, to name but a few.

But how does something as seemingly benign as being mindful or sitting in silence, help a business to run more efficiently and creatively?

Stress creates workplace fatigue, absenteeism, a lack of productivity, burnout and breakdown, as we are required to think of a million things simultaneously. As a result, we tend to have overworked 'monkey minds,' where our thoughts do not settle in any one place long enough to make an impact. No wonder so many poor decisions are made when the monkey is in charge!

"I served as senior advisor to Governor Schwarzenegger; it was eighteen-to-nineteen-hour days, seven days a week, working on every kind of imaginable issue needed to run a state," says educator **Bonnie Reiss**.

"Whenever I felt particularly stressed I would walk outside to Capitol Park. I'd go by a tree or sit on a bench, and meditate. I needed that five-or-ten-minute break in order to come back to myself. When I connect to that inner space then I get a greater sense of equilibrium and quiet. I can think more easily and make clearer decisions."

Moments of silence invite us to be present with ourselves. This helps us relax, yes, but it also creates a space where creativity, thoughtfulness, solutions to difficulties, better listening skills, and awareness of the bigger picture can emerge. Such moments decrease the effects of stress and increase our sense of connectivity.

Yet the opportunity to be quiet or self-reflective is sorely lacking for most businesspeople, their lives are normally so filled with activity and demands that agenda-free time simply does not occur.

"I was once teaching a business workshop in a big hotel," says mindfulness teacher **Jon Kabat-Zinn**. "As I entered the room, people were sitting around dressed in suits, reading the *Wall Street Journal*, cups of coffee in hand. I casually said, 'Why don't we just take a moment and sit quietly with no agenda?' I didn't give them any instructions; we just sat in silence for about ten minutes.

"When it was over, one of the executives said, 'You know, we never do anything without an agenda.' It was a real eye-opener for them to just sit and be still. We are usually so driven by all the doing that we soon forget who is doing the doing and why, and even what the doing actually is."

It would be highly presumptive to ask everyone in a business to meditate. However, there are ways to implement mindfulness, such as starting a meeting with a few minutes of silence (see below) or having a time-out room, which any business can do without having to call it meditation.

Some twenty years ago, we recorded an album at the Sounds True studio. In those days, the business was located in a couple of small rooms above a food store. Now Sounds True has sixty employees and a purpose-built building. They specialize in CDs and books on music, meditation, and spiritual teachings; they are the publishers of Deb's book, *Your Body Speaks Your Mind*.

One of the first things we noticed when we walked in was a meditation room, available for anyone to sit quietly, at any time. It is there because the owner knows the power of meditation to bring transformation.

"We started by publishing meditation teachings, and we wanted to ensure that our processes were equally as inspired. But the ancient teachers weren't living in a capitalist society, so they didn't have to answer this question as we do today," says publisher **Tami Simon**.

"We have a minute of silence at the beginning of all our meetings, even if it's between just a few people. Most people are moving from meeting to meeting or this conversation and that email, and when we get rushed we run over each other, we don't listen very well, we make bad decisions, and we are only half present. To just sit down for a minute clears the mind so that everyone is on the same page before the meeting begins.

"We learn to meditate 'on the spot,' in the midst of challenging circumstances and difficult conversations. When we apply the techniques (below) then we create a space for our own feelings, space for other peoples' feelings, and space for brilliance and originality to shine."

Here are three ways to bring meditation into the workplace, according to Tami Simon:

Begin Meetings with Silence

A busy day can feel like being on a non-stop train with one action item following the next without a break. Creating moments of silence, or moments of getting off the train, interrupts the tendency for habitual reactivity and drops us into the core of our being.

A simple way is to begin meetings with a few moments of being quiet together. People use this shared silence in different ways: to breathe and relax, to appreciate a few moments that are calm and spacious, or to let go of previous work concerns. These few minutes create a space that puts us all on the same page.

Attend to Sensations

If the mind is agitated, then the body is tense; if the body is tense, the mind will be agitated. By letting go of physical tension in the body, space is created in the mind.

In the midst of any interaction in which we are becoming impatient or agitated, we can bring our attention to the part of our body holding the tension. Internally scan the body from toes to the top of the head, zeroing in on any part that seems tight, clenched, or contracted. We may discover that our belly is in a knot or our shoulders are up by our ears, our hands feel like they are gripping something, or the bottoms of our feet are recoiling from the ground. When we discover an area of physical tension, we can use our in-breath to connect with that sensation. Then, on the out-breath, we simply release, relax, and let the tension go.

Bring Attention to the Back of the Body

Different physical and energetic postures carry different modes of being. If we want to exert and express ourselves and move forward into action, then we can bring our energy into the front of our body. If we want to make space for other people, listen deeply, and avail ourselves of creative ideas, then we can just lean back slightly and bring our attention to the back of the body.

In a meeting where everyone is interrupting one another and no one is being heard, it takes just one person to bring their attention to the back of their body, thereby introducing a quality of space and receptivity. This can change the tone and course of the meeting.

Taking The Plunge

As an example of taking meditation off the cushion, and in an attempt to help us confront and go beyond our limitations, doubts and fears, Rev. James Morton, the former dean of St. John the Divine Cathedral in New York, began an experiment:

> "He designed what he called The Plunge: an act of diving into unknown waters and getting completely whacked and disorientated so you can orientate yourself in a new way," says Roshi **Genro Gauntt**. "And he applied this to the street by sending his ministers out without any money, any place to live, or any identification, just like the homeless people they were serving."

From here developed the idea of street retreats: living on the street for a few days at a time without any resources, as a way to bring mindfulness into the midst of society's neediest, and by doing so to find a place of inclusivity. Participants have to beg or find food, get cardboard boxes or a place to sleep, and they meet during the day to meditate together, creating a ground of awareness.

> "Street retreats are where we live and practice meditation on the streets, begging and sleeping rough, just as any homeless person would," says Roshi **Bernie Glassman**. "We meet for meditation periods together and then disperse to do what we have to in order to survive, such as finding food to eat and places to sleep. I wanted to show that meditation is not just sitting on a cushion but reaches out to every aspect of life."

This added ingredient of meditation deepens the experience and the awareness that we are all a part of each other, that we are all equal, which includes acknowledging each other's existence, even if it is different to our own.

"I did the street retreat because I was so afraid of it," says actress **Ellen Burstyn**. "I could physically feel how much fear I had. The whole idea of having to beg was terrifying.

"The first time I begged, I had to cross a street to a restaurant with tables outside. Two women were eating there and I decided to approach them. As I walked toward them, I felt like I was crossing over some line that I had consciously never known was there; I was purposefully stepping through my ego to experience what was on the other side.

"I approached the women and simply asked, 'Excuse me, but I need a dollar for the subway. Could either of you spare a dollar?' The woman closest to me reached into her pocket and handed me a dollar without taking her eyes off her companion's face. I said 'Thank you' and walked away.

"I felt a strange pride that I had really accomplished something, but then enormous sadness as I realized that neither of the women had looked at me. I had got what I needed, but I had been disregarded, I had not been seen."

Doing anything outside of our experience is a plunge, especially stepping into places that we resist or are fearful of. We can take fear by the hand and get to know it. It doesn't matter what the plunge is, simply by going beyond ourselves we enter into a new paradigm. Ed took the plunge when we were on a beach in Rhodes, Greece.

"A tall crane at the far end of the beach was attracting a large crowd of people," recalls **Ed**. "Weaving our way through glistening bodies basking in the sun, we saw high above us someone about to bungee-jump. Fascinated, we watched him jump, bounce and fall again, until coming to rest a few feet above the beach. Immediately, I knew I was going to have to do it.

"The guy in front of me was nervous. I reassured him that all he needed to do was breathe and he would be fine. He was. He went up and he jumped. Then it was my turn and up I went.

"I stood on the edge of the platform, a large rubber band attached to my ankles, and my body simply wouldn't move. There was no inner programming, nothing in my brain that recognized how to cope with this situation. I knew I had to jump, but my body and mind both said no. Every time I wanted to jump, my body stood still. Nothing connected.

"Below me, a few hundred voices started shouting: 'Jump! Jump! Jump!' The minutes ticked by. And then something inside me simply surrendered, let go of resistance, released the fear, and I jumped.

"And beneath the fear, I discovered an enormous reservoir of sheer joy!"

Remember times you have met fear and moved through it, so many times when fear arose but you kept going: a new lover, a new job, childbirth. Fear may close the heart, but fearlessness comes from releasing resistance, and from heartfulness. Fear will stop us from facing our demons and participating fully in life, but fearlessness will jump off a crane into the unknown.

Contemplative Activism

We must come to see that peace is not merely a distant goal we seek, but it is a means by which we arrive at that goal. We must pursue peaceful ends through peaceful means. Dr. Martin Luther King, Jr.

Activism is dedicated to fighting injustice and bringing about social change. Is it any different if it arises from an angry reaction or from a contemplative and compassionate response? How does our behavior change with the awareness that we are not separate, but each is a reflection of the other? Does meditation make any difference when we are faced with extremes, like poverty-stricken prostitutes or machine guns?

We usually think of activism as being *against* something, whether it is war, torture, or dictatorial government, whereas contemplative activism is *for* something, such as fairness, freedom, and peace. This shifts us from maintaining the negative to supporting the positive. It gives us a whole new perspective, not just of activism but also of the deeper causes of injustice and violence. Where anger is exclusive and calls for further exclusivity, contemplative activism is inclusive, while informing us of when and how best to use anger, rather than being used by it.

> "Back in the eighties, I was an activist for a bunch of different organizations, but I was a horrible activist because all I did was project my rage," says yoga teacher **Seane Corne.** "I was the one with a soapbox and mega phone telling everyone how to live their lives. But it didn't serve anything.
>
> "What I realize now is how the world changes by embracing, not by pushing away. Rage pushes away; it

is a threatening energy that alienates. So, as an activist today, I invite by stepping in to the conflict and being as honest as I possibly can."

Here we meet the contradiction between being with what is versus the desire for change, between being at peace with whatever is happening while also protesting against it. This is the marriage of both passive and active, of being and doing. One of our meditation teachers said how we absolutely need to be at peace with what is, and that we absolutely need to protest and even shout out against injustice.

In the acceptance of what is, there is a spaciousness and nonattachment. Within that spaciousness, contemplative-based action has the chance to bring real change.

"We can create change through anger, but we can't create transformation through anger. The change will always revert back to something else," says yoga teacher **Rama Vernon**. "Meditation creates clarity of mind, and when we have clear thinking, our actions are more focused and we have greater power. If our minds are scattered, then whatever actions we take will only cause confusion.

"There may be moments when we need to use anger, but it is not the same thing as being angry. I have been angry with the KGB, as it was the right thing to do at the time, but I was responding with anger, not reacting. If we react with anger it can actually fuel a situation and we become part of the problem instead of the solution."

Ultimately, this is seeing wholeness in the broken parts, holding the vision of unity even as we protest the ignorance that is intent on destruction. In essence, nothing is broken, nothing needs to be changed, and completeness is present wherever and whenever we choose to focus on it. We hold that vision so that ignorance can have little leverage power.

> "Meditation is not just a matter of sitting quietly but of releasing the boundaries between self and other," says Sufi teacher **Elias Amidon**. "This can happen by sitting quietly, but it can also happen in the midst of action in the world. That's why I don't see any division between meditation and contemplative action. All activism involves engagement. We are responding to a call within us to care, to ease suffering. Contemplative activism seeks to bridge the gap of otherness between people."

Meditation and contemplative practices open our heart, letting in the pain of the world around us; they show us the reality of suffering and how each of us are an integral part of that suffering: if one person is in need, we are all in need. For Seane Corn, this awareness got her off her yoga mat and into action:

> "First yoga changed my body, then meditation changed my attitude," says yoga teacher **Seane Corn**. "Then I realized that whether my practice was fifteen minutes or four hours was irrelevant because it was not about how meditation can change me but how I, through this practice, can begin to change the world. What I really felt was how dare I not step into the world and hold that space?
>
> "I started by working with child prostitutes in Los Angeles. I met my shadow there. I hated those girls—and it wasn't just girls, it was young boys too—they were arrogant and defiant, but they were so wounded. They were also like a mirror in which I saw the part of myself

that had been abused, and how I hadn't dealt with my own defiance, arrogance or wounding.

"They really didn't accept me at first. Are you kidding? This big-mouthed, floppy-headed white girl from New Jersey, bouncing in to tell them how to do yoga? They slaughtered me! It was the most humiliating experience I've had because I went in trying to fix them. I didn't go in there recognizing that I *am* them. No way I wanted to go back! I sat in my car and cried and cried.

"The next time I went, I was way more humble as I'd recognized that we were there to serve each other. I have to love the wounded parts of myself: the prostitute, the impoverished, and the illiterate; I have to love myself so that I can hold someone else who is wounded.

"One day, I will never forget it, I walked into the shelter and there was this little Goth girl who had OCD and used to cut herself with razor blades. When she saw me, she jumped up and threw her arms around me. I was overwhelmed. Then, one by one, the other girls got up and hugged me. After that I had to come to the shelter ten minutes early to do the hug thing and I had to leave ten minutes late to make time for the hug thing. Because once we connected all they wanted was appropriate touch, to have a moment of holding that was safe.

"My next challenge was going into the field and meeting the children in third-world countries. I worked with Youth AIDS in the brothels in Southeast Asia. Teaching prostitutes about safe sex practices is really hard as they get $1 for sex with a condom but $2 without. If they use a condom then they run the risk of being raped, abused, or losing business.

"There was a porn house in the slum. I had to climb a ladder to get to it and force myself through this hole at the top into a pitch-black room filled with men. We'd interrupt their porn film and put on our own film about sexually transmitted diseases, and afterward we'd put their film back on and leave.

"It's one thing to sit at home and think how everything happens for a reason, but when I'm dealing with a fifteen-year-old prostitute who's dying of AIDS, then my own shit comes up. Like, this is unjust, unfair, and so very wrong. The rage flares up, but I know that I'd be no good for anybody if I came into this situation with judgment and anger.

"I can't presume to change anything. That's why meditation is so essential. It constantly brings me to a place of acceptance. Without it the rage would get too big; with it I have an open space to rest in."

Witnessing What Is

"Like activism, meditation wants to reveal the reality behind the illusion," says activist **Rabia Roberts**. "You begin to realize soldiers aren't necessarily heroes but victims. In the nonviolent worldview you can hold someone accountable but there's no blame for what is happening. If you are full of aggression and agitation, all you're doing is adding that negativity to the mix. That's why war can't bring peace."

Confronting our own doubts, limitations, and prejudices enables us to bear witness to places of pain or even torture. Logical understanding can't always be applied to what we see, as it takes us to a place of not-knowing. Whereas knowing something creates boundaries of identification and safety, not-knowing leaves us wide open, available and inclusive.

"I am often asked how I deal with people who have lost their limbs, children who have lost their parents, or women who take the lives of their own daughters to prevent them from being raped and abused," says educator **William Spear**. "The only way it's possible to witness this, other than totally numbing out, is to keep melting until I can expand my heart enough to embrace all that's in front of me.

"When I hold a child who's just lost everything she's ever known, or play basketball with guys who've had their legs cut off with chain saws and are tied to a board pushing themselves around, then I try to just be present and compassionate, even if it's unbearable.

"Meditation has been crucial in enabling me to be with people, for instance, who live in an area that's just been obliterated by a tsunami or earthquake. My practice is one of constantly opening my heart so I can be unconditionally present."

Contemplative activism arises from the awareness that we are no different from each other, that we are all victims of greed and hatred, and yet we also have the capacity to rise above this to a place of giving and caring. And, in its purest form, activism is simply bringing awareness and compassion to places of need.

The impulse to help others, to stand up against injustice, to make a difference in the lives of those who are unable to help themselves, and to do this in such a way that it doesn't create further harm, is an integral part of the contemplative life.

"When I was 21 years old I went to Nepal where I helped run a shelter for trafficked girls who had either escaped their traffickers, or there was a police raid in the brothels in Delhi or Bombay and we would go and get them," says activist **Kiri Westby**. "Some were eight years old or younger; some older ones had been in a brothel for years, forced to live in cages. Most of them were HIV positive.

"The most intense suffering is in an eight-year-old girl who's been raped continuously for longer than she can remember and who jumped out of a two-story building and broke her leg in order to get to the shelter, only to learn that it was her family who sold her to the brothel in the first place. And yet we could find moments of happiness and laughter together.

"I needed to meditate before I could even leave my room in the morning. It gave me the strength to rec- ognize that suffering is the human experience we all share and not to be overwhelmed by it, not to lose my balance. The suffering would have paralyzed me without that meditative space each morning.

"Then I worked with Urgent Action Fund for five years, traveling into war zones and witnessing stories of what was happening to women and girls. In the Congo, I had to cross a border that was just a tree log lined with fifteen-year-old boys holding machine guns. Often I would have money duct-taped to my stomach—cash for the women to take care of the kids—and I would have to convince these boy-soldiers that I didn't have anything on me. I couldn't meet them with even an ounce of fear or they would have shot me without hesitation. I got very good at dealing with boys with guns!

"More than anything else, meditation released me from anger. I would feel anger arise but I knew that the only way of surviving and working in this context was to let it go. There was no enemy; it was just a whole environment of people who'd been used and abused. I would constantly remind myself of their human qualities so that I could start the day without aggression."

Contemplative activism means dealing with our own aggressive tendencies, the violence within us, the anger, irritation, or moments of closed-heartedness. It is bringing mercy and tenderness to these places, to the wounded parts, so the war within us can heal. Compassion is the ability to be with another's pain and suffering, and we can do this when we have seen and accepted our own pain. Being a witness to atrocities and holding those who are in pain as close as we hold ourselves gives rise to ever-deeper levels of empathy.

"I was present at Nanjing, China, witnessing survivors speak of the Japanese who invaded Nanjing in 1937," says Roshi **Joan Halifax**. "In a matter of weeks, 300,000 people were massacred there. In addition, thousands of Chinese, from young children to old women, were raped, many of them in front of their families. Most were then killed but not all of them, and at this gathering at Nanjing one of the survivors, an elderly woman, testified about her experience.

"Sitting with the suffering, with my own response to listening to survivors and what they went through, and with the deep shame and remorse of the Japanese people, led to a tremendous upwelling of emotion within me.

"Compassion arises out of intimacy, not out of pity. In meditation, we can be present and feel deeply the suffering of the world, but not be annihilated by that suffering. We are actually able to bloom in its midst.

"That is what happened to me when I was in Nanjing. As difficult as it was to witness such suffering, what bloomed in me was an even more powerful resolve to work with my own mind, my own suffering, and with the suffering of others. Pity doesn't generate compassion, as pity is about there being a self and another, whereas compassion sees no separation."

Part Two
How To Do It

7 Doing It

*To go out of your mind at least once a day is tremendously impor-
tant, because.by going out of your mind you come to your senses.*
Alan Watts

Mindfulness

Essentially mindfulness is showing up in the present moment
with full awareness. It is becoming aware of yourself, how you
are in relationship with others, and how you are in the world.
It is being aware of the breath, and of moving. Nothing more.

Bringing mindfulness into your life implies you are living
more consciously, with other-centered awareness that is rooted
in kindness and compassion, rather than living with a "me" versus "you" mentality, which is rooted in dissatisfaction and fear.

Mindfulness can be done anywhere at any time by being totally
present in your world. It is both delightful and delicious to do!

Meditation

When you first begin meditating it can feel absolutely wonderful, peaceful, and full of visions or insights; or it can seem boring, difficult to focus, and uncomfortable. Thinking about what to cook for dinner or what to say at an imminent business meeting may follow a blissful, peaceful, or out-of-this-world session.

> "Meditation has always been simply (simply? Huh, I wish it were that simple!) the act of getting my mind focused in the present moment, without being influenced by the past or the future," says yoga teacher **Seane Corn**.

Meditation is a way of making friends with yourself. It will be no help at all if you feel you *have* to meditate, and then feel guilty if you miss the allotted time, or only do ten minutes when you had promised to do thirty. It is much better to practice for just a few minutes and to enjoy what you are doing, than to make yourself sit there, teeth gritted, because you were told that only 30 minutes will have any effect.

You may be beset with negative feelings, strong desires bubbling up to tell someone how much you resent them, or you may be overcome by feelings of warmth, tenderness and compassion. Just breathe into these varied feelings and let the emotions pass through.

> "Sitting there, doing nothing, just breathing, can be trickier than it sounds," says yoga teacher **Tara Stiles** on HuffingtonPost.com. "It may feel strange, uncomfortable, or even put you to sleep. Distractions try their best to pester you. Thoughts invade your aspiring-to-be-still mind. You start to fidget, adjusting your seat, clothes,

or hair, anything to have something to do. Meditation can be like a battle with yourself ... But if you stick with the uncomfortable moments, they will start to fade away and cool things will happen."

Remember those tedious piano lessons? Music needs to be played for hours to get the notes right, while in Japan it can take up to twelve years to learn how to arrange flowers. Being still happens in a moment, but it may take some time before that moment comes.

You practice to let go of the busy mind, of the stresses that keep the heart closed. You practice to open the heart without fear. You practice to come home to who you really are. Meditation is a gathering of your dispersed selves into one place. It brings you into the present moment and acts like an anchor, holding you in presence. It provides a structure for the mind to become focused and clear.

"There is a point in meditation where it becomes sweet. The beginning is like learning anything: you get on the horse, you fall off, and you get on the horse again. Practice, practice, practice!" says entertainer **David Shiner**. "Slowly, the joy of being in this quiet space becomes addictive. It's like the cream in milk that rises to the top. The real beauty of who we are, very slowly starts to bubble to the surface.

"Meditation has completely changed my life, completely transformed me as a human being. I think real change comes quietly and gently into our lives. You need to have patience and realize that anything of deep and lasting value takes time."

Almost everything we do in life is to achieve something: if we do this, then we will get that; if we do that, then this will happen. We are not used to doing something without a reason.

But in meditation you do it just to do it. For instance, if your purpose is to achieve a quiet mind, then the trying itself will only create further tension and distraction.

This concept of doing something just to do it is not an easy bedfellow. You want a purpose or meaning, some sort of reward, that your efforts are acknowledged, you especially want to be known as a great meditator! But holding on to anything, even a beautiful vision or mind-blowing experience, easily becomes food for the ego: *I* saw this white light, or *I* had this experience of being one with everyone. So even that has to go.

There was once a monk who had been meditating for many, many years, but he was discontented with his practice. He longed for a sign that he was doing the right thing. Finally, one day during meditation, he had a vision of a wonderful, shimmering golden Buddha that filled his whole mind. "At last,' he thought, 'this is it!'

He immediately went to tell his master: "Oh master, have I finally had the affirmation that I am doing the right thing? Is this the sign I have been waiting for?"

"Yes, yes," said the master. "This is very, very good. And if you keep meditating, hopefully it will go away!"

Meditation is more of an undoing than a doing. You undo the clutter and chaos in your mind, undo the past and let go of the future, undo the hold thinking has over you; basically you undo all the doing parts.

As thoughts and feelings come and go, everything is in constant movement. Yet there is also a deep quiet. In this way, both change and stillness are reflections of each other. Between them is an infinite spaciousness. You may only touch this spaciousness occasionally or know it fleetingly, or you may find yourself hanging out there.

"When you plant seeds in the garden, you don't dig them up every day to see if they have sprouted yet. You simply water them and clear away the weeds; you know that the seeds will grow in time," says bhikshuni **Thubten Chodron.** "Similarly, just do your daily practice and cultivate a kind heart. Abandon impatience and instead be content creating the causes for goodness; the results will come when they're ready."

The beauty of a regular meditation practice is the constant return to quiet and stillness in a world of noise and chaos. The term *coming home* is often used to describe this feeling, as if you are returning to a place you didn't know existed before yet which feels instantly and intimately known and familiar.

"Meditation gives us a taste of what it's like to feel good for no reason at all, and the more we do it, the less our happiness depends on external things and the more it deepens inside us," says singer **Krishna Das.** "It's just so cool because it works!"

There are various techniques that can help still the mind but these are not about trying to achieve anything or developing special powers, and no one technique is necessarily better than any other. Although the methods may differ, they all point to the same place, which is the cultivation of awareness.

The story goes that there was once a famous layman named Busol. He was deeply enlightened, as were his wife, his son, and his daughter. A man came to visit him one day and asked him, "Is meditation difficult or not?"

Busol replied, "Oh, it is very difficult—it is like taking a stick and trying to hit the moon!"

The man was puzzled and thought, "If meditation is so difficult, how did Busol's wife gain enlightenment?" So he went and asked her the same question.

"Meditation is the easiest thing in the world," she replied. "It is just like touching your nose when you wash your face in the morning!"

By now, the man was thoroughly confused. So he asked their son: "I don't understand. Is meditation difficult or is it easy? Who is right?"

"Meditation is not difficult and not easy," the son replied. "On the tips of a hundred blades of grass is the meaning."

"Not difficult? Not easy? What is it then?" So the man went to the daughter and asked her: "Your father, your mother, and your brother all gave me different answers. Who is right?"

The daughter replied, "If you make it difficult, it is difficult. If you make it easy, it is easy. Where are difficult and easy? Only in the mind. Meditation is just as it is."

Monkey Mind

I can't relax. I can't meditate. I just can't! My mind will not get quiet; it flies all over the place! My thoughts are driving me mad!

Sound familiar? Unfortunately, there is no direct route by which you start with a confused and chattering mind and end with a perfectly calm and serene one, never to experience distracting thoughts again. The mind is notoriously resistant to being quiet. You are going to be distracted, you will have thoughts. This is normal.

Within a few minutes of sitting you can experience a mind filled with meaningless nonsense, a body that starts to itch, ache, or want to move, or you will be disturbed by a dog barking, the sound of traffic, or a neighbor talking. Your focus can waver, you may float off in a daydream and forget where you are, or remember things to do that suddenly seem vitally important. Being so distracted, you may feel inadequate or no good at meditation, and so you quit.

"Meditation is not about getting away from it all, avoiding anything, numbing out, or stopping thoughts," says meditation teacher Lama **Surya Das**. "Without trying to be rid of thoughts or feelings, instead we learn to be mindfully aware of them."

The mind is like a monkey bitten by a scorpion and, just as a monkey leaps from branch to branch, so the mind leaps from thought to thought. Then, when you begin to pay attention, you find all this manic activity going on and it seems insanely noisy. Actually, it is nothing new, just that now you are becoming aware of it whereas before you were immersed in it, unaware that such chatter was so constant. It's like getting out of a car on the highway and realizing how fast the traffic is going.

> "Meditation helps us get quiet enough so that we can actually hear the ego at work," says actress **Ellen Burstyn**. "All the chatter is the ego's chatter, it's not the essence of our inner being. It's only when we settle down and get quiet that we can hear this voice clamoring for attention.
>
> "To me, meditation is quieting the chatter in the mind and that takes practice. I'm better at it on some days than others. Sometimes I sit down to meditate and the chatter just goes on and on and my whole meditation gets to be about going back to the beginning where I started."

After years of busy mind, years of creating and maintaining dramas, or years of self-centeredness, the mind is not always so ready to be still. It's not as if you can suddenly turn it off when you sit down to meditate; that would be like trying to catch the wind: impossible. But having a busy mind does not mean you can't meditate, it just means you are like everyone else.

You will judge yourself, your practice, and your progress or lack of it; you will criticize yourself, the technique, the teacher, your knees—the list is endless. You aren't expected to get it right every time, that is why it's called practice.

> "We see all these runaway thoughts that race through the mind, like 'I wonder if my car will be ready, is my parking meter overdue, will I get a ticket, should I get a new car, is my girlfriend happy?' Our minds are filled with these preoccupations," says Professor **Robert Thurman**. "But then we can just let them go and bring the mind back to itself."

It's impossible to fail at meditation. Even if you sit for twenty minutes and the whole time your mind is immersed in meaningless jibber-jabber, then that's ok. This will change, because the mind is constantly unpredictable: a busy mind now may be a quiet mind tomorrow.

One way to become more objective about thinking is to label the thoughts. Whenever you catch yourself drifting off into dramas or daydreams, you can silently repeat: *thinking, thinking,* and then come back to the practice. In the same way, if you are getting distracted, simply label it *distraction, distraction.* Each time you label *thinking* or *distraction* then you can let go; there's no need to struggle.

See thoughts like clouds in the sky, just moving through without stopping and without affecting the basic skyness. Or see thoughts like birds—beautiful, but here one minute and then gone. Watch them fly away.

Leave your front door
and your back door open.
Allow your thoughts
to come and go.
Just don't serve them tea.
Shunryu Suzuki

You don't have to stop the mind, just stop paying attention to it. Because then, in between the thoughts, comes what we call the gap. This is where true meditation takes place. It may start very small, but over time that gap will get bigger.

The meditations in this book give the mind an activity, so every time it wanders off on a thinking spree you can just witness this and bring it back to the present. This means gently training the mind to do something it may never have done before: to be still. Be gentle, be kind, be patient, and the monkey will tire.

Details

Sitting Right

An upright and straight spine is indicative of an alert open mind, whereas a slumped or rounded back can give rise to feelings of sadness and hopelessness—qualities you don't want to bring to meditation. So sit with a dignified, upright posture that reflects your self-respect. A straight back also enables you to breathe more easily. This is important, as many meditations follow the flow of the breath.

Traditionally, meditation is done sitting cross-legged on the floor, which some people can do easily. But for many others, their bodies are not used to sitting this way. In this case, an upright chair is just as good. The importance here is that you don't want an uncomfortable posture to distract you.

> "Just sitting cross-legged doesn't help us to become enlightened. Statues sit cross-legged; frogs sit like meditators and I don't think they are becoming enlightened waiting to catch a fly," says meditation teacher Lama **Surya Das**. "Awareness is the main component in meditation, the art of energizing and awakening consciousness."

If sitting on the floor, then use a firm cushion to lift the spine and buttocks, so the knees fall forward. In this position the back is naturally upright. If sitting on a chair, with feet flat on the floor, use a cushion to make sure the hips are slightly raised or your back muscles will soon be hurting. Despite a perfect posture, aches and pains do occur.

> "Many say the thing that mostly disturbs their meditation is discomfort in their body, maybe a pain in the

knees or in the shoulder," says author **Peter Russell.** "The normal reaction is to try to push it away, to get rid of it, to ignore it, or wish it wasn't there. But if you allow it in, you can start to explore it. Okay, there's a sharp bit here, a numb bit here, see how far has it spread.

"The actual hurt comes from the resistance of pushing it away. When we stop resisting, we stop pushing. We are just sitting with it as it is and then the pain starts releasing, muscles begin to let go. We don't have to get rid of something, rather let it in and let it be. And then the release happens of its own accord."

To sit comfortably, wear loose, relaxed clothing. Remove glasses or watch, undo any belts, turn off the telephone, and maybe leave a "Do not disturb" note on the door. In other words, remove anything that might cause a distraction.

When you first sit down, spend a few moments releasing any tension. Move your body back and forward a little to get a sense of balance and what a straight back feels like. Head is neither tilted up or down, but just resting comfortably. Eyes are either closed or slightly open but unfocused. Hands are resting in the lap or on the thighs.

One of our meditation teachers said that a strong and comfortable posture was 90% of meditation. This means a posture where there are no distractions, aches or pains. Most important is that you enjoy what you are doing, rather than doing it according to someone else's specifications. You are not trying to prove anything, or to achieve something. Meditation is there to connect more deeply with your sanity.

The Right Time

A lack of time is the main complaint we hear from people. Demands from home and work overlap and fill all the spaces.

With so much going on there seems to be little time for meditation. But this is the very reason to do it!

Think about what happens when your day is spent caring for or simply being there for others. How easy is it to get burned out, resentful or irritated? Or to feel stress building up inside? Does the quality of care that you offer become affected by that inner tension?

Taking time for yourself means creating a more easeful state that can only benefit all those around you; when you are feeling good then you can do far more than if you are dragging yourself through the day with little energy or in a bad mood. If your sense of inner balance is disturbed you can be of no help to anyone.

Have you recently noticed the smell of a flower or a bird soaring in the wind? If not, then it's time to stop.

As you let go of stress and connect with that quiet space within, then a beauty and joy arises. A stressed mind sees life as a burden or constraint; a relaxed mind sees life as a positive challenge and meets it with dignity and fearlessness

It helps enormously to set a time specifically for practice, such as when you first get up or before going to bed. This soon becomes a routine so that you don't have to think about when it sit. Meditation is cumulative, so the more often you do it, the more you will love it. Frequency is more important than length: five minutes every day is better than an hour once a week. Getting started is way better than thinking about doing it.

"A lot of people talk about meditation, but there's nothing that substitutes for daily practice," says Professor **Judith Simmer-Brown**. "Just putting your mind into some kind of settled, open, radiant space has a transforming effect that's way beyond any words about it.

"If you do five minutes a day then it will grow. It's the consistency of the practice that matters. We think going on a big retreat is going to change our lives, but that's like going into a cave with a bucket of water and throwing the water on the wall while expecting it to wear away the rock. What really wears away the rock is a daily drip."

Alone or Together

Whether to practice alone or in a group is a personal decision. We know people who much prefer to sit alone, as they feel able to enter into their own space more easily. But we also lead meditation group retreats and discover that most participants find it very supportive and inspiring to meditate together. The group energy seems to hold the space and allow everyone to go deeper into silence.

Those who do like to meditate with others often do so with a group of friends at someone's home.

"One of the best things I have done in my life was to start a weekly sitting group at my house," says author **Mark Matousek**. "It is a refuge and sanctuary for friends and deepens my relationships with these kindred souls. It serves as a kind of Sabbath in an otherwise hectic, secular life, an ongoing source of strength and joy from the simplest of practices."

Creating A Sacred Space

On the one hand, everything is sacred and wherever you are is no more important than anywhere else; on the other hand, having a place that is just for meditation creates a connection to sacredness in your everyday world.

"I visited the Ajunta caves in India," recalls **Deb**. "At the time of the Buddha, monks would retreat here during the rainy season; there are numerous rock carvings of them sitting or lying in meditation.

"When I was in one of the caves, I became aware of how very peaceful and quiet I felt. Then I walked outside and all my ordinary everydayness returned. Inside serene; outside ordinary. I went in and out a few times to check I wasn't imagining it.

"But no, it was the same rock, the only difference was that inside years of meditation practice had taken place. It reminded me of very old churches that have the same deep and pervasive quiet due to so many years of prayer and reflection."

A meditation space could be a room or just a corner of a room, the cupboard under the stairs or a closet: a place to have a cushion or chair to sit on, a blanket or shawl, a candle to bring light, perhaps some flowers, some incense, an inspiring or poetic book, or any objects that are important or meaningful. Creating the right environment is an on-going invitation to be still.

This can also be a place where any member of the family, including children, can go to be quiet and reflective; a place for anyone who is feeling upset or stressed and needs to chill out. It may become the most important room in the house!

Beginnings & Endings

It is good to be conscious of the beginning and ending of meditation.

To begin you can recite a short prayer or blessing, or a few words, such as, *My body is relaxed and easy, my mind is quiet and peaceful, and my heart is open and loving.*

At the end, you can spend a few moments in awareness of what has happened, creating any form of closing that feels appropriate, such as offering your practice to the benefit of all beings. Or you may prefer to say something like, *May all beings be well,* or *May all beings reside in calmness of mind and openness of heart.*

In this way you are acknowledging that what you do affects both yourself and others, due to your inter-connectedness with all beings.

Another suggestion, that many people do, is to chime a gong at the beginning and end of your practice. Or to hold your hands in prayer position and take a short bow, as a way of honoring all beings.

Helpful Hints

1. Start slow: Start with doing just three or five minutes at a time, once or twice every day. And commit to doing this for 30 days. By that time you will be noticing the effect.

2. Have a buddy: Find a friend you can do this with. They may live just down the road or on the opposite side of the planet, but just knowing they are also doing it can be very encouraging. Check in with each other regularly.

3. Move first if stiff or stressed: If your mind is in a fog, then do some stretching or yoga, gardening or dancing before sitting. By loosening your body you will loosen and relax your mind.

4. No wrongs or rights: It's normal to want to get it right. Remember, there are as many forms of meditation as people who practice it. There's no 'right' way to practice so there can't be a 'wrong' way.

5. Lighten up: It's so important not to take mindfulness and meditation too seriously; they're not a religion, just a way to find greater sanity.

6. Forget the details: It doesn't matter what the instructions are, just do it. Sit still for a few minutes every day. That's all.

7. Thinking is normal: We all have thoughts. Meditation is not about having an empty mind. It's about making friends with the thoughts you do have.

8. Do it anywhere: Mindfulness knows no restrictions. It can be practiced anytime, any place. Just be aware of yourself and your world.

9. This is a gift for you, a chance to just stop, breathe and relax into the moment.

10. Most happiness is transitory, but the real and lasting happiness is inside.

8 Sitting Meditation

Clear Mind Meditations

These meditations clear and focus the mind, bringing you into a still place. The different practices include Breath Awareness Meditation, otherwise known as Mindfulness Meditation, which focuses on the natural flow of the breath as it enters and leaves. This is also known in Sanskrit as *shamatha* meditation, which means calm abiding.

> "I would really suggest *shamatha* meditation," says spiritual teacher **Ponlop Rinpoche.** "The name itself, *calm abiding*, suggests that there are two stages here: first is calming your busy and emotional mind; and second is abiding in that state of calm."

Another Clear Mind meditation is Witness Meditation, where you become aware of the inner witness; you are aware without becoming what you are aware of. This is a very important meditation, as you gain great insight into both yourself and others.

Just Sitting Meditation is exactly as it says it is—just sitting. You sit with awareness of the world around you and awareness of the world within, without attachment or engagement. It opens you to great inner spaciousness and stillness. By resting in the present moment, you can expand your awareness to observe the mind itself, without getting lost in the content.

All meditation techniques are done sitting with a straight back so you can breathe easily and freely. Hands are resting in the lap. Eyes are closed or lowered.

Breath Awareness aka Mindfulness Meditation

> "The greatest discovery for me was that I could sit and watch my breath and that just breathing could become the most fantastically enjoyable experience I could possibly imagine," says philosopher **Tim Freke**. "And I thought if I can get this much pleasure just from breathing, then I'm okay, because as long as I'm alive I'm going to breathe. This was huge for me, this sinking into the breath in the body."

To clear the mind there is nothing simpler than watching the natural in-and-out flow of the breath. This is the foundation for all other practices, as it naturally brings your attention inward, enabling external distractions to drop away. The flow of the breath then takes your attention outward. In this way you are balancing your relationship between inner and outer.

You simply follow the breath as it enters and watch it dissolve and merge into your every cell, then follow the breath as it leaves and watch it dissolve and merge into the cosmos.

> "We can't breathe in the future and we can't breathe in the past," says Agape minister **Michael Bernard Beckwith**. "We can only breathe in the moment, so awareness of breath keeps us focused on where we are in the present. If we get caught up in worry, doubt, fear, or memories, then coming back to the breath breaks the train of thought and creates a gap where awareness can occur."

Remember to breathe naturally, not purposefully. If you start breathing too slowly or too quickly, then just stop for a moment until you regain your natural rhythm. The mind might become distracted and wander off into different thoughts, but the breath is always there to come back to.

"Just follow the breath and count to ten. But it's a hard thing to get all the way to ten!" says actress **Ellen Burstyn**. "When I first started doing it, I actually pictured the numbers. It gave me something to focus my mind on. I just paid attention to my breath and pictured the numbers, got to ten and started over at one. It helped me because it's hard to get quiet and just breathe without having something to do."

Practice:
Breath Awareness Meditation aka Mindfulness Meditation

Establish your posture, take a deep breath and let it go.

1. Now bring your attention to the rhythm of the breath and simply watch your natural breathing, without trying to change it in any way.
2. Let your breathing be easy and relaxed, attention is still and focused. As you maintain awareness, let yourself rest in the rhythm of the breath.
3. If you find you are getting distracted or caught up in thinking, simply label your thoughts as distraction or thinking and let them go; or see them as birds in the sky and let them fly away.

Do this for at least five or ten minutes. Just breathing and being. When you are ready, take a deep breath and gently open your eyes.

Here are further instructions so you can focus more fully on the breath and be less distracted:

1. Focus your attention on one of three places, whichever is most natural to you: either on your nose tip, watching the point where the breath actually enters and leaves; in the center of your chest, watching it rise and fall with each breath; or in the belly, about an inch below your navel, watching the belly rise and fall.
   a. Become familiar with all three places. If at any time you feel restless or caught up in your thinking, then bring your attention to the breath in the belly; conversely, if you are getting sleepy or soporific, then bring your attention to the breath at the nose tip.
2. To help deepen your concentration, silently count at the end of each out-breath: breathe in, breathe out, one; breathe in, breathe out, two; breathe in, breathe out, three; continue to count in this way up to ten, and then start at one again. If you lose the count or go beyond ten, just start at one again.
3. Alternatively, with each in- and out-breath, you can silently repeat, *breathing in, breathing out*; or just *in, out*. This keeps your mind flowing with the breath.

Witness Meditation

Where Breath Awareness meditation is like calming the surface of the water, essential for developing a state of quiet abiding, Witness meditation is like looking through the water to see what lies below.

The witness sees without becoming engaged. This is the core of meditation. By developing the witness you realize you aren't your thoughts or emotions. You have them, you appreciate them, but you are not them.

"Meditation is recognizing that I am awareness witnessing sensations and thoughts," says philosopher **Tim Freke**. "When I recognize this, I experience a profound sense of oneness with everything and everyone. They are not separate from me any more than space is separate from the things it contains."

Witness meditation takes the concentration you have developed by focusing on the breath and expands it further. Instead of a single focus you now have multiple inputs and witness whatever is there. This allows you to see the transitory nature of all things—here one minute and gone the next—and the inherent impermanence that lies beneath.

In this meditation you let the mind be as it is, without judgment or discrimination. All kinds of thoughts may arise, or feelings and sensations. Just be with them, watching, without pushing away or holding on. In between the thoughts or sensations there is stillness, a gap where the mind rests and natural insight arises.

Practice:
Witness Meditation

Relax your body and take a few deep breaths. Begin by focusing on your breath, letting your mind settle into the rhythm of the in and out flow.

1. Now become aware of how the quality of each breath may change, sometimes long, sometimes short, deep or shallow, and notice the pauses between breaths. You are not trying to do or achieve anything, simply to stay present and aware.

2. Now notice any physical sensations that arise, such as an ache or a desire to move. Name the sensations: hot, cold, stiff, relaxed, tight, warm, or soft. As you observe, watch what happens to the sensations.

3. Now watch as thoughts or feelings arise. Name the feelings: sad, happy, angry, or peaceful. Watch what happens as you acknowledge them.

   If you realize your mind is wandering, name it as wandering. Sometimes you will only become aware after you have been thinking for a while. Do not judge or condemn yourself, this normal.

4. Notice mental and emotional sensations and name them: fear, anxiety, doubt, irritation, restlessness, boredom, depression, or joy. Just watching, just witnessing.

   Watch the arising and dissolving, the coming and going of each breath, of each sensation, thought or feeling. Stay open and present. As you observe the moment, so the truth of that moment will become clear.

When you are ready, take a deep breath and let it go. Gently open your eyes.

Just Sitting

There are no real instructions here. Just find your seat, take a few breaths to quiet your mind, and settle into the wakeful awareness of just sitting.

This meditation takes everything you have already established: the calm abiding of watching the breath, and the witness awareness. Then it drops all objects of focus and receives everything that comes into the field of awareness: thoughts, feelings, sounds, sensations, and breathing.

Here you sit with no agenda, no judgments, no doubts, just resting in awareness of all. This asks that you let go of anything that is unnecessary, such as expectations, desires, impressions, or concerns. You just sit.

"Meditation can mean really being focused on something, or it can mean letting go of all focus and simply being still," says spiritual teacher **Gangaji**. "It's not a matter of saying, 'I am going to meditate,' it's more like 'I am just going to be here for a moment without doing anything, without following any thought.'

"And in that there is peace, a surrendering of the mind's activity to this huge vast silence and spacious awareness. It's not anti-mind activity; simply that usually the mind is spinning round and round, so it's a stopping of that spin."

Open Heart Meditations

Here are meditation practices that open the heart by focusing on and developing qualities such as loving kindness, compassion, and forgiveness. As you practice these forms of meditation you go from *trying* to be kind or compassionate to *becoming* them, fully embodying these qualities so they become natural reflections of who you are.

> "When we get quiet and still we are able to see how we are all interconnected. We don't stop at our skin; we are all a part of each other," says author **Mirabi Bush.** "There is absolutely no reason to keep our heart closed at all, ever."

An open heart is peaceful, joyful, loving and forgiving, because these qualities already exist within you. Meditation simply enables you to connect with them.

Loving Kindness

Loving Kindness, also known as *Metta* meditation, is a powerful and transformative practice. It awakens the awareness of and care for both yourself and others equally, while also recognizing that there is no essential separation.

The meditation practice leads you through different stages, from developing this quality toward yourself, your loved ones, to people you may be having a hard time with, and finally to all beings. This follows the opening and expansion of awareness from self-centeredness to other-centeredness.

Specific phrases can be repeated to encourage this quality; these are not a request but statements of actuality, such as: *May I be well, may I be happy, may all things go well for me,* and *may I be peaceful.*

The beauty of these phrases is both in the self-affirmation, and that you can use them all the time, wherever you are. Going to the doctor: *may I be well.* Going on a date: *may I be happy.* Going for an interview: *may all things go well for me.* Feeling stressed: *may I be peaceful.* Being criticized by your boss: *may she/he be well.* Sitting in a crowded train: *may all beings be happy.* Stuck in a traffic jam: *may all beings be peaceful.*

Practice:
Loving Kindness Meditation

Spend at least five minutes on each stage of this practice. If you find it easier, focus on just one person each time you practice.

Start by focusing on your breath, and flowing with the in and out rhythm. Then bring your attention to breathing into the heart-space, in the center of your chest. With each in-breath feel your heart-space opening and softening; with each out-breath release any tension or resistance.

1. Now either repeat your name or visualize yourself in your heart-space so that you can feel your presence there. Hold yourself there gently and tenderly, like a mother would hold a child. Feel a growing sense of friendliness and love for yourself.

    Silently repeat: *May I be well, may I be happy, may all things go well for me, may I be peaceful.*

    Become aware of any resistance—any reasons why you should not be well or are not worthy of being happy. Acknowledge these feelings and let them go.

    May I be well: Feel this in your body, especially places where you are not well.

    May I be happy: Bring into your heart any unhappy feelings, and accept and love them.

    May all things go well for me: Bring into your heart those places that are not going well and let the loving kindness change and uplift them.

    May I be peaceful: Bring into your heart any stress and worry and transform them into peace.

2. Next, bring your loving kindness to your nearest and dearest—your family and friends. One by one bring them into your heart as you visualize them or repeat their name.

    Direct your loving kindness to them, as you silently repeat:

    May you be well, may you be happy, may all things go well for you, may you be peaceful.

    Breathe out any conflicts or disagreements you may have, and breathe in happiness and joy.

3. Now bring your loving kindness to someone you do not know or have no feelings for: a neutral person. Open your heart to this unknown person as you repeat:

May you be well, may you be happy, may all things go well for you, may you be peaceful.

As you do this, you begin to realize how it is not the personality that you are loving, but the very essence of beingness, and this you share. Together you walk the same earth and you breathe the same air.

4. Now direct your loving kindness toward someone you are having a hard time with, whether a friend, relative, or colleague—anyone where communication is not flowing and there is misunderstanding.

   Keep breathing out any resistance and breathing in openness as you hold this person in your heart and repeat:
   May you be well, may you be happy, may all things go well for you, may you be peaceful.

   Be careful not to get caught up in reliving the details of the story, for these are irrelevant. You are focusing on the essence of this person, not what they did or didn't do. No shame or blame, just awareness and openness. Wish them wellness and happiness.

5. Now expand your loving kindness outward toward all beings, in all directions. Open your heart to all, whoever they may be, silently repeating: *May all beings be well, may all beings be happy, may all things go well for all beings, may all beings be at peace.*

   Let go of any prejudice or resistance. Feel as if kindness is radiating out from you in all directions, like the ripples on a pond. Breathe in loving kindness, breathe out loving kindness. All beings are worthy of being loved, whoever they are.

   Repeat: *May all beings be at peace, and may I be at peace with all beings.*

When you are ready, take a deep breath and open your eyes, letting the love in your heart put a smile on your lips.

Compassion

Normally, we prefer to focus on as much good and to let go of as much bad as possible. However, there is another way that is the exact opposite. This is the Tibetan meditation practice known as *tonglen*, the practice of receiving and giving, otherwise known as Compassion meditation.

This is a practice of breathing in pain and suffering, inhaling resistance or fear into the heart, where it is transformed into joy, healing, kindness, and compassion. Then this positivity is breathed back out into the world.

Tonglen has the remarkable effect of making you stronger. It sounds like it would weaken to inhale such pain and suffering, but it does the opposite. Rather than turning away from suffering—feeling too sensitive to be exposed to it, or too weak or fearful to withstand it—you welcome it all to come in. You experience it, taste it, touch it, but the suffering doesn't stay. Instead, it is transformed.

This gives you the power to transform any difficult feeling or situation. Every time you see or feel suffering, whether in yourself or in another, every time you make a mistake and are just about to put yourself down, every time you encounter confusion or difficulty, every time you see someone else struggling, upset or irritated, you can breathe it all in and breathe out acceptance, caring, and loving friendship. You can offer this to whoever needs it, including yourself.

Just a few breaths of tonglen will bring armfuls of compassion into any situation.

Practice:
Compassion Meditation

Start by focusing for a few minutes on the natural flow of your breathing. You use the breath as the basis for this meditation.

1. With each in-breath, inhale all the pain and suffering of yourself and others, all the sadness and fear. You can focus on a particular person, on a group of people, or on all beings.
2. Take this suffering into your heart and immediately transform it into tenderness, kindness and compassion. Then exhale all that goodness out into the world.

When you are ready take a deep breath, and take the compassion with you into your daily life.

Forgiveness

> "Every night before I go to sleep, I say, 'I forgive every-
> one, including myself.' I don't want to have a slate full
> of unforgiven things before I go to sleep. It is like doing
> your dishes before you go to bed," says Rabbi **Zalman
> Schachter-Shalomi**. "And then on Sabbath I go over
> the whole week and forgive everything that has hap-
> pened, whether I did it or someone else did it."

Forgiveness is vital in a world that encourages rejection and revenge.
This is a powerful meditation that releases feelings of guilt, blame,
and shame, leading you through three stages from forgiving yourself,
forgiving another or others, to asking for forgiveness.

This is not about rehashing the details or the story, of who
did what or who said what to whom. Those details are well
known. There has been pain, but this meditation is about
seeing the ignorance that the deed or words arose from that
caused the pain. This ignorance you can forgive.

You can also contemplate what forgiving yourself or someone else would mean. What emotions would be released? What
old remorse or long-held grudges? What pain that you are so
used to you had forgotten was there? Jealousy, anger, or sadness? What changes in your life would occur? The freedom to
dance, or to love??

Forgiveness can take time; your experience will deepen
the more you do the meditation practice. Move into forgiveness gently, perhaps just doing one step of the meditation
in each session.

Practice:
Forgiveness Meditation

Spend five to ten minutes on each stage of this practice. If you wish you can focus on just one stage at a time.

Start by bringing your attention to your breathing. Let your breath open and soften your heart-space as you breathe in, and release any resistance as you breathe out.

1. Now focus on yourself, repeating your name or visualizing yourself in your heart-space. Hold yourself there with care and tenderness. You have put yourself out of your heart, so now is the time to embrace yourself.

    Silently repeat: *I forgive myself; I forgive myself. For any harm or pain I may have caused, whether through my words or my actions, I forgive myself.*

    As you do this, you may feel shame at what you have done, or how you have betrayed yourself. Acknowledge this, and then let it go with each out-breath. The story is not important.

    Keep breathing in softness, inviting forgiveness.

    Repeat: *I forgive myself, I forgive myself.*

2. Now focus on a person you wish to forgive, someone you have put out of your heart. Bring in to your heart-space an image of this person or repeat their name.

    Breathe out any resistance, and breathe in openness and softness.

    Silently repeat: *I forgive you. I forgive you. For the harm and pain you have caused, through your words and your actions, I forgive you.*

    Let your breath relax you. Be gentle with yourself. Do not get sidetracked by the story or the details of what happened, of who said or did what. The story is irrelevant.

Breathe out any reasons why this person should not be forgiven, and breathe in forgiveness.

Repeat: *I forgive you, I forgive you.*

3. Now visualize in your heart-space someone you may have hurt or upset, someone who has put you out of their heart. Now allow yourself to be forgiven.

Silently repeat: *I ask for your forgiveness. I ask for your forgiveness. For the hurt or pain I may have caused you, through my words or my actions, please forgive me.*

Keep breathing out any resistance. You can put down the story and let go of the shame or the guilt, it is irrelevant.

Feel your heart opening to receive forgiveness.

Repeat: *I am forgiven, I am forgiven.*

Feel the joy of forgiveness throughout your whole being. You have forgiven. You are forgiven. Rejoice in the release. When you are ready, take a deep breath and let it go.

Appreciation

This is an important meditation to generate deep appreciation and gratitude for your breath, your body, your ancestry, and your world. You can generate appreciation for anything, whether animate or inanimate, alive or passed. Such appreciation and gratitude expands the open heart.

> "Gratitude is a gracious acknowledgment of all that sustains us, a bow to our blessings, great and small, an appreciation of the moments of good fortune that sustain our life every day. We have so much to be grateful for," says spiritual teacher **Jack Kornfield**.
>
> "It is not sentimental, not jealous, nor judgmental. Gratitude does not envy or compare. Gratitude receives in wonder the myriad offerings of the rain and the earth, the care that supports every single life."

Practice:
Appreciation Meditation

Spend a few moments focusing on the in-and-out flow of your breath.

1. Now develop an appreciation and gratitude for the cushion or chair you are sitting on, thanking it for supporting you in your meditation. Honor the people who made your seat, and thank all the elements that were involved in the making of it.

   Repeat: *For your service, your work, and your sacrifice, I am grateful.*

2. Now extend your appreciation to the building around you, feeling gratitude for its protection and safety, for the space it provides in which you can meditate. Silently thank those who made the building, and the materials that were used.

    Repeat: *For your protection, attention, and your generosity, I am grateful.*

3. Now extend that appreciation to the ground beneath you, always there to support and sustain you. Feel a deep gratitude for this earth, for the trees, plants, animals, birds, the oceans and fish.

    Repeat: *For your abundance, your variety, and your care, I am grateful.*

4. Now extend your gratitude to your body, appreciating how it deeply cares for you, how it is within this body that you experience meditation. Honor how your body is a part of the food you eat, the water you drink, and the air you breathe.

    Repeat: *For your wellness, your kindness, and your care, I am grateful.*

5. Now extend that appreciation to your parents, for without them you would not have this body and would not be here now, sitting in meditation. Honor however much or little they gave to you as being the most that they were capable of.

    Repeat: *For your kindness, your love, and your sacrifice, I am grateful.*

6. Now extend that appreciation further back, to your grandparents and then your distant ancestors. Between them all they gave you the color of your hair, the shape of your eyes, the laughter in your voice. They passed on

to you their knowledge so that you may grow greater than them.

Repeat: *For your gifts, your sacrifice, and your wisdom, I am grateful.*

7. Now bring your appreciation and gratitude back to yourself and to your breath. Become aware of the flow of your breath entering and leaving, and deepen your appreciation of the life it gives you.

Repeat: *For your constant giving, and for the life you give me, I am grateful.*

Now take a deep breath, and take that appreciation with you into your daily life.

Two-Minute Meditations

The unexpected power of meditation can be seen in just a few minutes of being still and breathing. Two minutes is all you need to quiet your mind, still your emotions, and find your balance again.

If you can commit to either two or maybe five minutes every day, and do this for a month, then meditation will naturally grow in meaning. It becomes a part of who you are. It will lead to a deep mindful awareness and inner peace, giving rise to sweet moments of happiness.

Meditation doesn't have to be done in the right posture, at the right time, or in the right place. It can be done anytime and anywhere—including the bathroom, a bus stop, the train, a park bench, sitting at your office desk, or while the kids are playing. If the bathroom is the only place where you can be alone, then don't hesitate. Just lock the door, sit on the seat, and breathe!

"A mini meditation happened recently when I was in the line at the DMV, the Department of Motor Vehicles," says actor **Ed Bagley, Jr.** "I didn't bring a book, I didn't have an iPod, no crosswords, nothing, and then I realized this was a gift! I could breathe in and breathe out. I was standing in line meditating and it was no longer about getting to the end of the line, but just what was happening right now.

"We can get a full meal when we sit and practice more formal forms of mediation, but then there are snacks available that we can get in line at the DMV."

Anytime Practice

Anytime you feel stress rising, your mind going into overwhelm, or your heart closing, just find a place to be quiet and focus on your breathing.

As you breathe, do one of the following:

1. Repeat*: Soft belly, soft heart* with each in- and out-breath
2. Breathing in, repeat: *I calm the body and mind;* breathing out*: I smile.*
3. Breathing in, repeat: *I am easeful and peaceful;* breathing out: *I am love*

Just Being Meditation

Find a comfortable place to sit, and close your eyes.
Become aware of yourself, of your presence on the chair in the room.

1. Follow the flow of your breath as it enters and leaves. You are breathing ... sensing ... heart beating ... feet on the floor
2. Be present with whatever is happening in the moment
3. Sit and breathe ... just sitting ... just being
4. Silently repeat: *May all things be well, may I be at peace with all beings*

When you are ready take a deep breath and gently open your eyes.

Stop and Pay Attention Mindfulness

1. Every two hours throughout the day, just stop what you are doing and look around you. Breathe, smell, and be aware of this extraordinary world you live in.

2. Notice how easily your mind takes you into thinking, dreaming and dramas, past or future fantasies—anywhere than just being here now.
3. Listen to the layers of sound.
4. Breathe into the present moment.

Breathing Meditation

Spend a few being aware of the room around you and the chair you are sitting on.

1. Now focus on your breathing, watching the natural movement of air as you breathe in and out. Silently repeat, *Breathing in, Breathing out.*
2. If your mind starts to drift just see your thoughts as birds in the sky and watch them fly away. Then come back to the breath.
3. Silently repeat, *I am here, I am now, I am present. I am here, I am now, I am present.*

When you are ready, take a deep breath, open your eyes, and smile!

Soft Breath

Find a comfortable place to sit. Close your eyes and feel your body relaxing.

1. Silently repeat, *Soft breath, soft belly. Soft breath, soft belly.*
2. Follow the movement of the breath from where it enters at the nose tip all the way to the lungs or even the belly.

When you are ready, gently become aware of your body and of the room around you, and take a deep, grateful breath.

Anytime Loving Kindness

Breathe into your heart, softening and relaxing with the in breath, letting go of tension with the out breath.

1. Now hold yourself in your heart and silently repeat: *May I be well, may I be happy, may I be filled with loving kindness.*
2. Now wish all beings around you be well, wish that they be happy.

Take a deep breath and take that loving kindness with you wherever you go.

Walking Mindfully

You can walk along a country road, a city street, in the office, or the back yard. You can walk slowly, normally or fast—whatever you need.

1. As you walk become aware of the movement of your body and the rise and fall of your feet.
2. Silently repeat: *lifting... placing* with each step.
3. Before you finish, just stand absolutely still for a few moments with your eyes closed, then resume your day.

Loving Your World Meditation

Find an upright meditation posture. Spend a few moments just breathing.

1. Now extend appreciation to your body, how it cares for and nourishes you. Honor the food you eat, the water you drink, the air you breathe, the clothes you wear.
2. Now feel a deep gratitude for the chair you are on, thanking it for supporting you. Honor the person who made it, and all the elements that were involved.

3. Now extend appreciation to the ground beneath you, always there to support and sustain you
4. Now bring your appreciation to your breath. Become aware of the flow of your breath entering and leaving your body.

Now take that appreciation with you into your life.

One-pointed Visualization

This practice hones your awareness. Start by becoming one with your breathing.

1. Now visualize and focus on an object you deeply love, such as the sea or a tree.
2. Bring all your senses into play: smell the object; feel the object; taste the object; hear the object; and see the object, so that you become one with it.
3. Keep breathing. Rest in your awareness.

When you are ready, take a deep breath and let the visualization fade.

Open Heart Meditation

Bring your attention to the heart space in the center of your chest and breathe in and out of this space. With each in-breathe feel your heart gently opening and softening. Silently repeat, *May heart is opening and softening.*

Stay here as long as you wish. When you are ready, Take a deep breath and let it go. Take the peace of your heart with you throughout your day.

9 Moving Meditation

Body Awareness

Meditation is not a matter of either ignoring or forgetting the body. We can move, walk, run or dance with both the mindfulness and the awareness that we bring to sitting. Moving meditation is found in hatha yoga, tai chi, qigong, swimming, walking, running, dancing, and more.

Emotion and movement both arise from the same Latin root: *emovere*. To be emotionally moved by something is to be physically affected by it. If we are sad or depressed, then our movements will be heavy and slow; if we are angry, they become jerky and dramatic. Moving the body beyond its habitual limitations loosens energy on both the physical and psycho/emotional levels. In other words, releasing tensions in the body also releases them in the mind.

Feelings and memories get locked in the joints, muscles and ligaments, often from as far back as childhood. The joints join up our thoughts and feelings with our actions, enabling us to move with grace and fluidity. If movement is restricted or blocked then energy can't flow freely, leading to a lack of emotional ease. So by moving the body, greater freedom comes to the mind.

"Sitting, as a way of strengthening, focusing, and enlightening the mind, is only one of the steps," says spiritual teacher **Sakyong Mipham**. "The next step is meditation in action, so that you embody the practice. This is more challenging as you have activity going on at the same time as stillness. You have to balance the two.

"When you bring your mind back and draw it into the center of your heart, you become more synchronized and awake to your immediate environment."

During long periods of sitting meditation, such as on a retreat, the periods of sitting are always combined with periods of walking meditation, as a way to not only move and stretch the body but also to apply meditation into the rest of life. The challenge here is that the eyes have to be slightly open to see where you are going, and this can give rise to greater distraction. But by surrendering to the walking, so the boundaries between stillness and movement dissolve.

"We use the body as a tool for concentration and focus," says yoga teacher **Kali Ray.** "Being aware of the movement in every posture shows us how to be aware of every movement or action in life. The body is like an instrument used by a musician, a play between the breath and the posture in a steady rhythm. We start to feel this rhythm in life as a rich, meditative flow."

Yoga

The word *yoga* literally means "yoke," or "that which unites." It unites the body, mind and spirit and brings this relationship into balance and harmony. Developed thousands of years ago, yoga has many different aspects: ethics, discipline, relaxation, devotion, and meditation, as well as hatha yoga, a system of physical movements. This is the form of yoga practiced the most in the West. Hatha uses different postures or *asanas* to stretch, invigorate, balance, and tone the body. As the body finds greater equilibrium, so does the mind.

> "My initial impression of yoga was that I would just do a few asanas, a few postures, to kind of un-stress all of my nerves, and then I would just sit down and go into deep meditation," says yoga teacher **Richard Freeman.** "If only it were so simple! I still see it as dissolving back into meditation and awareness, but it's also a way of taking the insight gained in meditation out through my nervous system and into the world."

Although some forms of hatha yoga are now taught in an energetic or very hot fashion, traditionally it was done slowly, with total awareness. Ed trained in India, where he was taught hatha as a meditative flow. The system of asanas was developed so that each posture relates to a different attitude, expressed both physically and mentally. The movement helps the spine become supple, release tension, and focus the mind inward. The effect subtly changes the way you move or walk, as well as calming the way you think and feel.

Yoga is ideally suited to relieving stress and as a result it is taught in many stress-reduction clinics. But it is especially important for recognizing limitations and being able to go further. Without pushing or straining, you can breathe and move through your resistance to a posture, simultaneously watching the mind going beyond its own restrictions. Each different posture stretches both body and mind in a different way, so as you move into different positions they shift your reference points and open you to a new understanding.

This is meditation in movement that helps deepen your sitting meditation experience. Yoga enters into every aspect of your life and becomes a living meditation finding expression through the body. As the body opens, you open; as the body flows, your resistances release and relax into that flow.

"I teach the *vinyasa* form of yoga, defined as 'things going in a logical sequence.' There are three parts to this: rising, abiding, and dissolving," says yoga teacher **Cyndi Lee**. "The dissolving of one thing is the arising of the next... we inhale and exhale, and that is a vinyasa; every day and night is a vinyasa; every life is a vinyasa; every ebb and flow of the tides is a vinyasa.

"We can observe the same flow with any kind of feeling: it arises, it abides, it dissolves. At the end of the day, it's not about how long we can sit on our mat or whether we can wrap our legs around our neck, it's how much we can open to ourselves and other people."

Walking

Alistair was having a hard time sitting. We were leading a five-day meditation retreat in Ireland, and Alistair's posture was askew. He would start out sitting upright but within a few minutes he'd be bent over. Every so often one of us would quietly say, "Sit with a straight back," and he would try, but it didn't last long. However, when we interspersed sitting with walking meditation, Alistair was in his element, with a soft smile on his face.

At the end of the five days we asked how everyone had done and if there was anything they would like to share. When it was Alistair's turn, he simply said, "Thank you for introducing me to my feet."

This meditation is not the same as going for a walk through the woods or by the beach, lovely as that may be. It is a more focused, deliberate, and conscious walk. The eyes are open but lowered just to the ground in front, so that the mind does not drift or get distracted but you can see where you are going. Entering into the rhythmic movement of walking, of just placing one foot in front of the other, allows the mind to find a natural stillness.

"Walking meditation is probably more effective for me than most other meditations, as the thinking mind starts to drop away when I come into body and feeling. It also softens that sense of me, I, and myself," says psychotherapist **Maura Sills.**

"I start to pay attention to movement in relationship, to make contact with the earth, to feel my body in space; I pay attention to the air. You can't go walking with your eyes closed; you have to have some sense of external awareness as well as inner awareness. The relationship of the two is essential."

Walking meditation is a practice of balancing the outer world with the inner one, with the feet as the bridge between the two. As your mind becomes quieter and there is just walking, with nothing else going on, then you will find you are merging into the rhythm, feeling each small movement, and the effect it has on your whole being.

"I was barefoot and had been walking slowly in meditation across the lawn," recalls **Deb**. "I had stopped and was standing very still when this worm crawled out of the earth and traveled across my foot before disappearing in the grass. I've never liked worms that much, but in that moment I felt intense gratitude that it had deemed me safe enough to walk over, and then I suddenly became it, there was no difference or separation between us. I too disappeared into the grass."

This practice can be done outside or inside, wearing shoes or barefoot. It can be done continuously, or in a space of maybe thirty to fifty steps with a marker at each end, which you walk between. This decreases distraction and eliminates any concern about where you are going.

Retreat 2001
It was the edge of winter at first
before warmth creeps into the ground
before apple blossom redbud and dogwood
before trees find their leaves

It is here we lost our edges
silent vigil in slow motion
as cardinal vireo and wren
sang us into spring
JULIE CARPENTER

Practice:
Walking Meditation

This can be done for anything from ten to thirty minutes.

1. Stand upright with your hands held lightly together in front so that your arms stay relaxed. Your eyes are lowered, but not your head, so you can see the ground in front while not being distracted and without getting a stiff neck.
2. Begin to walk, bringing your awareness to the movement.
3. As you walk, silently repeat with each step: *lifting... placing.*
4. Move slowly, or a little quicker if you need energizing. Stay mindful and aware, keeping shoulders and neck relaxed, your movement flowing and your breathing natural. *Lifting... placing.*
5. Become aware of the meeting point of your feet with the ground: notice the bumps and dips, the texture and quality of the ground. *Lifting... placing.*
6. If you need to turn around, then first stop for a moment and notice the difference between moving and stillness. Walk. ..stop...turn...stop...and then walk again. *Lifting... placing.*

At the end of the walk, stand completely still for a few moments, watching your breath and feeling the sensations in your body. Enjoy the stillness!

Running

Exercise of any form has the potential to bring the mind into the body and, in so doing, to create an inner quiet. Deb experiences this when she swims. For her, it is a wonderful meditation: the quiet of the water, the movement of her body, her mind completely still. Running is another form of exercise that can be experienced as meditation.

"The truest form of meditation is sitting, because your body is in a natural balance between being awake and being very still," says spiritual teacher **Sakyong Mipham**. "When you are running or doing moving meditation, the mind has to become very precise in order to fully embody the movement. When I'm long-distance running, my meditation is a combination of the movement of the legs, the feet, the breathing, the sense of being centered, and the immediacy of the situation.

"Some people listen to music while they run, but I'm very focused on being present. When you are present with your breathing, the pain, or whatever else is going on, then there's a fullness of the whole experience. You are very alive in that process.

"When running and entering 'the zone,' you get completely synchronized and the mind opens. Time becomes irrelevant.

"In Tibet, we say the mind is like a rider on a wild horse. Wherever the horse goes, the mind has to go. In an untrained mind, they say the rider is helpless, he doesn't have any legs and arms and can't control the horse. We experience this when we are sitting in meditation and our mind is just wandering everywhere. Then the horse is taking us all over the place. When we are running with awareness and we're focused in the present moment, then everything becomes totally awake. We are in control of the horse! It's a wonderfully clear space."

Dancing

Dance is used in all the spiritual traditions as a form of losing the self and opening the heart to merge with the divine. It is seen in the Sufi whirling dervishes, the Tibetan dancing lamas, the ecstatic dance accompanying Hindu devotional chanting, or in Jewish circle dancing. It brings us together as one, releasing the boundaries that separate.

> "We were eating dinner at a small taverna on the Greek island of Rhodes, when we heard the waitress talking about a dance to be held that night," recalls **Deb**. "It was midnight before the entire village had assembled on a flat, grassy outcrop normally used for playing football: small children, lanky teenagers, farmers, shopkeepers, grandmothers, and old men clinging to walking sticks, they all came. Tables had been spread with food and drink. A small band began to play. Over the next two hours we watched both the young and old hold hands and dance, sometimes in circles, sometimes in winding lines, sometimes in pairs or groups of eight.
>
> "I experienced the power of this collective dancing when one of the teenagers, who had rings in his ears and nose and tattoos all over his arms and who at first had looked completely bored and disinterested, stepped into the middle of the circle and led a snake-like dance around the field, his eyes alight with joy."

Dancing is an immediate and effective medication for sadness, depression, despair, or for anything that holds back happiness and openness.

To dance is to feel the joy of each breath and the gift of life in your veins. This is particularly true of free dance, where the body moves of its own volition, self-consciousness dissolves, and in its place comes an awareness of each part of the body in relation to the whole. Dance enables your self-imposed limitations, inhibitions, fears and self-obsessions to be released; in their place, you find a greater sense of delight and freedom.

"Stillness is my rhythm," says dance teacher **Gabrielle Roth.** "In my teens, alone in my bedroom with the radio turned up as loud as possible, I danced my pain—all my unexpressed sadness. Much later, I would try to find a way to get out of my head and the fastest way to still my mind was to move my body. Put the psyche in motion and it heals itself.

"Normally, the mind is thinking one thing, the body is moving in a different direction, and the heart is doing a third thing, so there's a huge disconnect. We live in the chat room above our necks, but we need to find our roots and our center through our body."

Practice:
Dancing Meditation

1. Little instruction is needed here. Chose your favorite music and let it rock you.
2. Try different rhythms: fast, melodic, staccato, soft, and slow. See what it feels like to open your chest, to lift your arms, to spin or bend, to move quickly or slowly.
3. Keep breathing throughout. Let your emotions ebb and flow with the rhythm.
4. Dance your feelings, your relationships. Dance your illness or your pain. Dance your anger; dance your grief; dance your fear. Then dance your joy and laughter!

And then stop and be still. Stand or sit and just breathe gently and enter the stillness that is always there behind the movement.

10 Sounding Meditation

Letting The Heart Sing

"I was asked to create a musical bridge between the opposing forces of Protestants and Catholics in Northern Ireland," says singer **Chloe Goodchild**. "We were part of a peace program, and this was the moment when the Dalai Lama was going to walk the peace walk, which basically divides the Protestant and Catholic communities.

"We were there to chant the mantra to Tara, the sacred hill that was the ancient seat of the high kings of Ireland. Tara is also the great Goddess of Compassion in Buddhism.

"The paramilitary had agreed to a ceasefire and were standing within about fifteen yards of us with raised guns. The plan was to have the Dalai Lama open the peace gate in the peace wall, but I was advised that what often happens when they open the gate is that the children from the two opposing sides start throwing stones at each other.

"The Dalai Lama had started walking down the street lined with thousands of people. I was told it would be about 20 minutes before he reached us, as he kept stopping to talk to people, so we just kept chanting.

The wonderful thing about the delay was that it gave both the paramilitary and the people waiting a chance to join in the recurring melody line that was praising their sacred hill.

"The rain stopped and the sun came out, the peace gate was opened and the Dalai Lama walked through. The children who normally throw stones at each other were singing; both sides were chanting the Tara mantra. It was totally awesome."

Such a moment of harmony in a war-torn county is a wonderful example of how a shared sound takes us beyond differences to a place of oneness. This unifying of our voices creates a powerful form of meditation, taking us out of the habitual mind and into a place of deep resonance, both within ourselves and with each other.

The sound does not need to make sense in order to unite the minds of the ones who are singing. But such accord can be lost if the thinking mind intrudes: if you understand the words then you are easily distracted by them, and are no longer present. Deepesh Faucheux experienced the effect of a change in language during his time as a Catholic monk:

"Gregorian chanting was designed to be a meditation; research shows that the Gregorian frequency works on the brain to elevate it to a spiritually altered state," says therapist **Deepesh Faucheux**. "When we chanted, I would get very high, even transported.

"It was always a chant done together, what is called *ecclesia*. The frequency of the sound integrated the behavior of the chanters, smoothing out the rough edges of anger or fear. When we sang Gregorian it was like Prozac, elevating our mood.

"Such sounding together made many of the petty things that happened in a community of monks seem totally unimportant. It actually made life in the monastery bearable, sometimes even blissful, and was the only therapy the monastery needed.

"Gregorian chant was written for the Latin language, but when they tried to do it in the local dialect then many of the monasteries and convents fell apart. The residents started fighting with each other. They had lost that shared integrative quality."

Whether through singing or chanting, shared sound blends not just our voices but also our vibrations, which promotes healing on many levels. At the same time, the hormone oxytocin is released, which increases the feel-good factor. This hormone is best known for its role in inducing childbirth, but it appears to also influence the ability to bond with others and maintain close relationships. Sounding together loosens the barriers of separation, which allows for a healing of both cells and souls.

"I have a formula, which is frequency plus intent equals healing; sound coupled with consciousness creates the outcome of the sound," says sound therapist **Jonathan Goldman**. "The mystics and physicists have always known that everything in the universe is in a state of vibration. When we sound, then every part of the body is in resonance. This includes our brain waves, breath and heartbeat. By attuning together, our nervous systems attune and entrain with each other."

To heal on an inner level is to become whole, a bringing together of all the different parts of both your psyche and body. The health of your mind directly affects your physical health; repressed psychological and emotional issues are often at the root of stress and illness. True healing has to start with the mind in order to bring balance and harmony to the body. Sound can be the source of that healing.

"I was lost for eleven years. I got addicted to cocaine. I was like a burnt-out building," says chanter **Krishna Das**. "In 1994, I was standing in my front room in New York and suddenly I knew that if I didn't start chanting with other people, putting my ass out there in a public way, that I would never access the dark corners of my heart. I knew chanting was the only tool I had available. As a result, that front room is now easier to live in."

Making Sound

To benefit from the meditative quality of sound does not mean you have to sing in tune, let alone have a perfect voice, for the intent to chant is way more important than whatever sound you are capable of making. The meditation is through the voice and the breath coming together, when you enter into a spontaneous experience of inner resonance.

> "When we sound, then oxygen starts moving and changing the biological system to relieve stress and emotional burdens," says sound therapist **Vickie Dodd**. "Sounding dissolves thoughts like *I can't do this; I'll never know how to do it; I'm tired; what time is it? I need to go; I'm uncomfortable.*
>
> "We can sound such thoughts; we can sound unpredictable, chaotic, politically incorrect thoughts. All the different characters inside of us need a voice. When we sound then oxygen starts moving through us, changing our biological system to relieve these emotional burdens. Then they can settle down, they have been heard."

Although there are many forms of sound that can be used, from the single "ah" to more traditional mantra chanting, humming is one of the simplest and most direct sound experiences that we can all participate in.

> "Humming is really easy and anyone can do it," say musicians **Deva Premal and Miten**. "You don't have to be able to sing, or to know any mantras; you just hum with closed lips. You take a deep breath so that you are filling your lungs, then you hum to the end of

that breath, and then you take another deep breath and you hum.

"If you hum for five minutes, and then sit in silence for five minutes, you will have an experience that is going to be felt throughout the day. The sound of humming synchronizes your spirit with your body. It brings you into a silent space.

"Humming is something anyone can do for ten minutes each morning: five minutes humming, five minutes sitting silently."

Sounding does not always imply making a vocal sound; we can be as deeply moved through playing and making music, whether it be a meditative instrument, such as a flute or piano, or one not usually associated with inner silence, such as drums.

"I love the silence, but for me it is the silence in music," says musician **Kitaro**. "What is music and what is silence? Both are meditation. Sounds are waves and this is meditation, and the silence of meditation is filled with sound.

"Every August full moon, at the base of Mount Fuji, I drum all night long for twelve hours, and this is a very deep meditation. The drumming becomes a wave of movement through me; it gives me deep inspiration and strength. The concentration combined with the rhythm means my mind goes in and out, it changes all the time, sometimes I close my eyes and even in a concert I am far away. Sound goes out, and silence goes in."

Making sound also confronts you with the ego, and with your desire to be identified as the singer or chanter, rather than surrendering the ego by becoming one with the sound. In surrendering, you can be moved beyond the music, the repetition of words, or the intoning of chants, to a place of emptiness that is filled with vibration.

"How do we become the sound?" says sound therapist **Jonathan Goldman**. "By clearing out the ego. Otherwise, we may be making the sound, but we are not one with it."

Sound is also about listening, whether to music, chanting, the sounds of nature, a bird singing, or perhaps the rhythm of a washing machine. Achaan Sumedho, a Buddhist monk, told us how he was once teaching meditation in Bombay and right outside was a construction site. He had just started the meditation when a pneumatic drill began digging up the road. He could not stop the program, so he simply said, "Became the sound."

In the same way, we once had a motorcycle revving up outside the window during a meditation class. Nothing to do but become the sound!

"We think we can't be quiet because of the sound of the refrigerator, or of the traffic," says author **Peter Russell.** "But actually the sound is just a part of being in the present moment. It is our resistance to sound that is the barrier to meditation. If we don't resist it, then the mind can be quiet in the middle of all sorts of noise."

When you drop down beneath the top layer of sound, beneath what you know, then a deeper listening occurs, one that extends your awareness. Listening is itself a meditation.

"I use sound to quiet my mind, to quiet the chatter, so that I can go deep enough to listen," says sound therapist **Vickie Dodd.**

Chanting Sacred Sounds

Mantra meditation consists of repeating a sound or series of sounds, either silently or out loud, over and again. The word *mantra* means a sacred sound and is composed of two elements: repetition and freedom, implying that through the repetition of the mantra you will find your freedom.

For a busy mind, repetition encourages one-pointed awareness, and for a sleepy mind it gives something to focus on. In this way, as you become absorbed and anchored in the sound, the mind is released from its agitated thinking or habitual patterns, discovering the stillness within. It is like a broom that sweeps the mind free of clutter.

Mantras are common to all religions and spiritual traditions. Sanskrit mantras were first experienced by the Hindu sadhus or holy ones while they were in deep meditation, and then taught to their disciples.

A mantra may be a word or the name of a spiritual being, such as *Mother Mary, Jesus, Allah,* or *Namo Buddha.* Or it may be a word or phrase that has special meaning to you, such as *Shalom* or *Be at Peace.* In Eastern traditions, *Om* is a favorite sound, as it means the sound of the universe; *Om Shanti* is peace; *Om Mani Padme Hum* is the Jewel in the Heart of the Lotus; while *Om Namah Shivaya* is homage to Shiva, who dispels negativity. The recitation of the name of *Krishna* is said to take you out of the material world and into the joy and salvation of Krishna Loka, the land of milk and honey.

In mantra meditation, you can use any of these sounds, such as repeating *Om* as you breathe in and *Shanti* as you breathe out. Keep it simple and easy to repeat. Treat it like a friend you keep close.

> "Each person can use the mantra 'I am loving awareness.' Just repeat this and become loving awareness,"

says spiritual teacher **Ram Dass**. "Then we share that loving awareness with all others."

The mantra can be repeated silently or out loud, either during your meditation session or at any time during the day. Deb loves chanting silently to herself as she is shopping as it stops her buying stuff she doesn't need!

Repetition is considered the most direct way to calm the mind. Mantra meditation is like spiritual food: it awakens your creative process, nourishes your spirit, and opens your heart. What more could you want?

Ed learnt chanting when he lived in India. While on a teaching tour a man asked him to come to his home to see his ailing wife. As he entered their simple hut, Ed chanted a healing mantra—Om Namah Shivaya—over the woman's bed. She immediately lit up with a big smile as she grasped his hand.

Practice:
Mantra Meditation

Take a few deep breaths and relax.

1. Now begin to repeat a mantra, either silently or intoning it out loud. Repeat it in rhythm with your breathing.
2. Use the mantra as an anchor to keep the mind focused and quiet. Whenever you get distracted or drift off into thinking, just bring your mind back to the sound.
3. You can also use a rosary or mala—a string of 108 beads—as a way of keeping your mind focused. With each repetition of the mantra, move one bead.

After chanting for a few minutes or longer, then just enjoy being silent and still for a few minutes.

Part Three
The Fruits of Silence

11 Finale

The future is a concept—it doesn't exist! There is no such thing as tomorrow! There never will be because time is always now. Alan Watts

No Solid Self

When Deb was a teenager living in London, her mother was the editor for *The Middle Way*, the journal of the British Buddhist Society. As a result, Deb met some fascinating people, such as the Zen philosopher Alan Watts, who was writing the foreword to her mother's book when he died, and Douglas Harding, the author of *On Having No Head*, who had spontaneously stopped thinking and realized, therefore, that he had no head:

> "I stopped thinking. Reason and imagination and all mental chatter died down. It was a vast emptiness vastly filled, a nothing that found room for everything—room for grass, trees, shadowy distant hills... I had lost a head and gained a world." **Douglas Harding**

Many of us experience this feeling of no-head, or no-mind, in those moments when a sense of ourselves as a separate, identifiable individual seems to disappear or merge with everything around us. It's as if boundaries have dissolved and in their place we become the clouds in the sky and the birds singing and the tree and the flowers at the foot of the tree. For Deb's mother, Anne, this happened when she was washing the dishes and heard the sound of a wild bird song. In that moment, she became the sound and lost any sense of being separate from it.

An experience of no-mind can occur when we contemplate, 'Who am i?' Most people believe, "This is me, this is my body, I see myself very clearly." We identify ourselves with our thoughts and feelings, believing they constitute "me," just as we think that our body is "me."

> "I use inquiry as a way of getting the mind to turn inward to the silence," says spiritual teacher **Gangaji**. "It could be the question, 'Who am I?' Or, 'Where is silence?' Rather than sending the mind outward to gather information, it is sending the mind inward to question our basic assumptions of who we think we are."

Our attachment to form is due to the concept that there is a separate you and a separate me, and all emotions, both negative and positive, grow out of this assumption of duality. And on a relative level this is true. But is it possible to find a "me" that exists independent of anything else?

> "Of course, if someone asks, 'who are you,' then we tell them our name. But if we really investigate from the outside inward, layer by layer, through every part of the body until we reach the heart, we will never find the 'I' as a solid thing to which we can point and say, this is me," says **Tai Situ Rinpoche**

When we presume that our solid self is separate from anything or anyone else, others are seen as "not-me." But when we understand that the self is impermanent, constantly changing, interconnected and interrelated, we see that not only is there no solid "me" but there is no solid "you" either.

> "I thought inside was a solid Bob, that there was a solid Bob-person in here, but when I look for that Bob, I can't find any such thing. Bob is a word; it is a name only. I am empty of a solid Bob, but I am full of the incredible rich process of body and mind as multiple perspectives and angles," says Professor **Robert Thurman.**
>
> "The material like this table that I can put my knuckle on now is just as much emptiness as the air between my knuckle and the table where my hand is poised. There is no absolute solid, and there is no absolute intangible. When you look for the solid core of anything, you will find only emptiness, or non-duality."

The great Indian sage Ramana Maharshi taught through stories. One of our favorites, which we often share in our workshops, we call *The Movie Theater*. Ramana explains that when we go to a movie theater, and before the movie starts, we see a blank screen. Then the lights go out and the projector goes on, the movie plays, and the drama begins. We feel sad or happy, angry or uplifted by all the emotions in the movie. Then the movie is over, the projector is turned off, the lights go on, and again there is the blank screen. Ramana says that the blank screen is like our consciousness that is empty of content, while the dramas are the feelings that play out in our mind.

In a similar analogy the mind is likened to the sky that is inherently empty. It contains clouds, rain, tornados, thunder or lightning, sunshine and stars, but behind all these various manifestations, the sky is always there. In the same way, we contain anger, grief, fear, joy, happiness, yet we are not them. Everything from even a few minutes ago has already dissolved. Everything from yesterday, last week, or last month no longer exists. Thoughts and feelings arise and hang around for a while and then go.

Non-duality, the wisdom of no-mind, appears when there is no longer a sense of "me" or "me-ness," no ego-bound person where the "me-self" is the center of the universe. With no awareness of "I," there is just awareness. When we meditate we go deeper within. It is there we discover that we are not the mind, nor the content within the mind, but the vastness of no-mind.

"Meditation for me is an amazement that whatever I am contemplating is there at all," says author **Anne Bancroft**. "How incredible that spring comes and the grass grows, or that a cup of coffee awaits me on the table, even that a table exists! It is awareness of the miracle that anything is. And I experience that it is, before I come to what it is. It is totally important in my contemplation to be filled by that it is.

"But whatever the mystery of its beingness, the table also has a conventional existence here and now, an existence within language. So the second part of my meditation is to do with knowing its everyday life: a table that is both a mystery and a table that is here and now."

Form and Emptiness

We live in a world that appears very real: I see the trees, I hold a glass, I drink my tea, and the oceans are not in the sky. From this perspective, *form* applies to everything solid, graspable, and real.

Emptiness, on the other hand, implies an absence of anything meaningful, a state of nothingness that we do our best to avoid. It is identified with fear and loneliness, even despair. Emptiness is something that is felt somewhere in the pit of our belly, and a lot of time is spent trying to fill this inner hole, to find meaning and to feel connected.

When we experience form and emptiness in meditation, however, a very different picture emerges. This one sees the inherent limitation in thinking of form as solid and real, as well as the delusion that emptiness is either meaningless or void. Instead of solid, the world of form appears transient and impermanent. Rather than being a dull void, emptiness appears rich, full, and inclusive of everything.

So these two meanings of form and emptiness are like two sides of the same coin. But the terminology can be confusing.

"I was teaching emptiness and someone asked me, 'Does that mean your chair is also emptiness?'

"I said, 'Yes. Everything is emptiness,' says spiritual teacher **Ponlop Rinpoche**.

"So then he asked, 'Then how can you sit on the chair? Why don't you fall right through?'

"So I explained that he was mixing the two truths. He was putting my relative body on an absolute chair. This is a pillar, and that is the lawn, and this is a tree. We all agree on that, there's no debate, no argument. Just as long as we don't look too closely, that works perfectly fine. But as soon as we do look closely, then not even modern science can find anything solid and tangible; there is just emptiness."

On a relative level our form is all we have; we appear very solid and we take that appearance very seriously. But while our form may seem to be immutable and unchangeable, our true nature is free, completely unbound and unfettered. We are both empty and full at the same time. Relative mindfulness is the awareness of form and all the identifiable things in our world, while absolute mindfulness is the awareness of emptiness, which is our true self.

"It is the emptiness in the cup that makes the cup valuable, because into the emptiness we can put our tea," says spiritual teacher **Jack Kornfield**. "It is the empty space in the room that allows us to move around. All things come out of emptiness.

"Form and emptiness are two sides of this mystery of existence itself. When we only focus on the world of form, we suffer. When we let go and rest in spacious awareness, we find a grace and wisdom."

By enquiring, "Who am I?" we realize there is no fixed, discernible form that equals the "I." Yet, while empty of a separate self, we are also full of everything, for all things are contained in every other thing. Form becomes both form and formlessness, while emptiness, or no-mind, is full of each intricate aspect of existence.

"A few months ago, I understood, suddenly, how thought was just an illusory thing...And then I wondered who is it that's aware that I am thinking?" says actor **Jim Carrey**. "Suddenly I was thrown into this expansive, amazing feeling of freedom from myself...I was no longer a fragment of the universe; I was the universe."

On The Road To Nowhere

While writing this book we spoke to well over a hundred meditators from all walks of life, such as Christian ministers, Zen monks, Tibetan lamas, film actors, authors, activists, motivational speakers, the list goes on. But they all had one thing in common: their experience of meditation was unique to each one. What religion they believed in or what films they had starred in were irrelevant. Meditation was the most abiding and rewarding.

Embarking on a path of personal transformation is laudable, yet the journey may be far from smooth. There are numerous routes complete with detailed maps and signposts but still we may get lost, take a wrong turn, or have to ask for directions. Great headway may be made, only to find we are back at the beginning, or wonder if we are even on a path at all. It can be like a roller coaster ride or a walk in a gentle glade.

This journey is full of unexpected glimpses of joy and deep happiness. It is a journey without beginning or end. Rather than a definable goal, there is continual discovery, with each discovery worthy of the entire journey.

And so we awaken to the greatest journey of all. It takes place right now, as all that has ever happened or will ever happen is found in just this exquisite moment. There is nowhere to go and no way to get there, as we are already here. It is arriving home to our own true self, to our inner sanity, to who we have always known was there but hadn't looked deep enough to find. The treasure at the end of this journey to our heart is the love that is the source of our deepest peace.

Wake up, rejoice, you are that love you seek!

About Ed and Deb Shapiro

Bestselling authors Ed and Deb, winners of the 2010 Nautilus Gold Book Award, are columnists for **HuffingtonPost.com, Awaken.com, Care2.com, and others.** They are the authors of 20 books on mindfulness, meditation, personal development, and the bodymind relationship, published in many languages.

Ed and Deb lead mindfulness and meditation retreats and personal development workshops worldwide, and are corporate consultants and personal coaches working with CEO's and senior management. They have been teaching together for 30 years.

Ed was a New York City dance champion born in the Bronx, who became a yogi, skier, skydiver and bungee jumper. Deb is from the English countryside, the granddaughter of Sir Winston Churchill's speechwriter and editor. While Ed trained in New York with Swami Satchidananda, and later in India where he became Swami Brahmananda, Deb was doing Zen retreats with Jiyu Kennet Roshi, and then training with Tai Situ Rinpoche. She is a Bodymind expert.

www.EdandDebShapiro.com

Ed, left, as a Swami in India

The Dalai Lama with Ed and Deb at his residence in India

Shapiro books and meditation downloads include:

YOUR BODY SPEAKS YOUR MIND, *Decoding the Emotional, Physical, and Spiritual Messages That Underlie Illness.* Winner of the **2007 Visionary Book Award** in Alternative Health, finalist for the 2007 Nautilus Book Award. In over 18 languages.

BREATH AWARENESS MEDITATION – Deb Shapiro
This meditation focuses on the natural flow of the breath, or mindfulness of breathing. You relieve stress and anxiety, become more aware, and connect to inner peace. Guided Meditation for calming the mind and greater clarity.

WITNESS MEDITATION – Ed Shapiro
Witness Meditation is the awareness of thoughts, feelings and sensations without attachment, awakening insight and awareness. This Guided Meditation invites you to be fully present in this moment.

LOVING KINDNESS MEDITATION – Deb Shapiro
Awaken deep kindness, warmth and compassion toward both yourself and others. Includes positive affirmations for healing any conflicts. Develop friendship and loving kindness to all. Guided Heart Meditation.

FORGIVENESS MEDITATION – Deb Shapiro

With a forgiving heart, we transform negativity; any wrong that has been done is released from its emotional hold. Guided Meditation for forgiving yourself and others, letting go of fear or anger, and finding your true peace. Forgiveness is the greatest gift you can give yourself.

YOGA NIDRA – Inner Conscious Relaxation – Ed Shapiro

Yoga Nidra releases deep-rooted stress and unconscious trauma. This invites a dynamic relaxation and healing, leading to profound inner peace. Guided Relaxation for body and relief of tension.

YOGA NIDRA – Journey Through The Chakras – Ed Shapiro

Guided journey through the seven chakras, awakening levels of perception. This frees your mind and opens the heart. As you deepen relaxation, you become vital and creative.

Available from: EdandDebShapiro.com

Contributors Bios

Elias Amidon, author, teacher of the Sufi Way. *See* sufiway.org

Judith Ansara, teacher of applied human consciousness. *See* sacredunion.com

Anne Bancroft, author *Zen: Direct Pointing to Reality*, and *The Buddha Speaks.*

Marc Ian Barasch, author *Field Notes on the Compassionate Life*, founder Green World Campaign. *See* greenworld.org

Michael Bernard Beckwith, author, minister, Agape Spiritual Center. *See* agapelive.com

Ed Begley, Jr., actor and environmental activist. *See* edbegley.com

Sylvia Boorstein, co-founder Spirit Rock Meditation Center, author *Pay Attention for Goodness' Sake. See* sylviaboorstein.com

Joan Borysenko, author *Minding the Body, Mending the Mind. See* joanborysenko.com

Gregg Braden, author *The God Code* and *The Divine Matrix. See* greggbraden.com

Ellen Burstyn, academy award–winning actress, author *Lessons in Becoming Myself. See* ellenburstyn.net

Mirabai Bush, The Center for Contemplative Mind in Society. *See* contemplativemind.org

Michael Carroll, business consultant, author *Awake at Work. See* awakeatwork.net

Jim Carrey, award winning actor, activist, and green environmentalist.

Pema Chodron, nun, author, director Gampo Abbey. *See* pemachodron-foundation.org

Seane Corn, ambassador for YouthAIDS, activist, yoga teacher. *See* seanecorn.com

Richard Davidson, professor psychology and psychiatry. *See* psych.wisc.edu/faculty/bio/davidson.html

Deva Premal and Miten, musicians, singers and chanters. *See* devapremalmiten.com

Vickie Dodd, sound therapist, author. *See* sacredsoundsschool.com

Deepesh Faucheux, psychotherapist, transpersonal psychology at Naropa University. *See* naropa.edu

Jane Fonda, award–winning actress, social and political activist. *See* jane-fonda.net

Debbie Ford, author *The Dark Side of the Light Chasers*. *See* debbieford.com

Matthew Fox, Friends of Creation Spirituality, author *Original Blessing*. *See* mattewfox.org

Richard Freeman, yoga teacher, Yoga Workshop in Boulder, CO. *See* yoga-workshop.com

Tim Freke, The Mystery Experience teacher, author. *See* timfreke.com.

Gangaji, spiritual teacher, author *The Diamond in Your Pocket*. *See* gangaji.org

Grover Genro Gauntt Roshi, co-foundeer Zen Peacemaker Order. *See* zenpeacemakers.org

Bernie Glassman Roshi, founder of Zen Peacemakers, author. *See* pecemakercommunity.org

Jonathan Goldman, director Healing Sounds Association, author. *See* healingsounds.com

Joseph Goldstein, co-founder Insight Meditation Society, author *Insight Meditation: The Practice of Freedom*. *See* dharma.org

Chloe Goodchild, singer, musician, author *The Naked Voice*. *See* thenakedvoice.com

Tara Guber, founder Yoga Ed., for educational benefits of yoga. *See* yogaed.com

Joan Halifax Roshi, abbot Upaya Zen Center in New Mexico. *See* upaya.org

Andrew Harvey, author, founder the term *sacred activism*. *See* andrewharvey.net

Gay Hendricks, author, Foundation for Conscious Living. *See* hendricks.com

Jean Houston, Foundation for Mind Research, Mystery School, author. *See* jeanhouston.org

Jon Kabat-Zinn, founder Mindfulness Based Stress Reduction. *See* mindfulnesscds.com

Byron Katie, founder The Work, author *Loving What Is*. *See* thework.com

Kitaro, Grammy and Golden Globe winning musician. *See* kitaromusic.com

Jack Kornfield, founder Insight Meditation Society and Spirit Rock Meditation Center, author *A Path wit Hearth*. *See* jackkornfield.org

Krishna Das, internationally known chanter and musician. *See* krishnadas.com

Megan Cronin Larson, play therapist, yoga teacher, meditator. *See* avibrantmindllc.com

Cyndi Lee, author *Yoga Body, Buddha Mind*. *See* cyndilee.com

Noah Levine, meditation teacher, author *Dharma Punx*. *See* noahlevine.com

Mark Matousek, writing teacher, author *When You're Falling, Dive*. *See* markmatousek.com

Mingyur Rinpoche, author *The Joy of Living. See* mingyur.com

Ponlop Rinpoche, Buddhist teacher, author *Mind beyond Death. See* nalandabodhi.org

Ram Dass, spiritual teacher, author *Be Here Now* and *Still Here. See* ramdass.org

Kali Ray, yoga teacher, founder of TriYoga®. *See* triyoga.com

Bonnie Reiss, senior advisor to California Governor Arnold Schwarzenegger. *See* bonniereiss.com

Marshall Rosenberg, Center for Nonviolent Communication. *See* www.cnvc.org

Linus Roache, stage and film actor, nominated for a Golden Globe, long-time meditator.

Rabia Roberts, social activist, co-director Spirit in Action. *See* boulderinstitute.org

Gabrielle Roth, creator 5Rhythms, author *Maps to Ecstasy. See* gabrielleroth.com

Peter Russell, author *The Global Brain,* and *From Science to God. See* peterrussell.com

Sakyong Mipham Rinpoche, spiritual teacher, author *Ruling Your World. See* mipham.com

Jeff Salzman, director Boulder Integral, CO. *See* integrallife.com

Ed & Deb Shapiro, meditation teachers and authors *Your Body Speaks Your Mind* and *Merging. See* EdandDebShapiro.com

Rabbi Zalman Schachter-Shalomi, founder P'nai Or and Alliance for Jewish Renewal. *See* www.rzlp.org

David Shiner, clown, actor, playwright, director Cirque du Soleil. *See* cirquedusoleil.com

Maura Sills, co-founder Karuna Institute UK, director Psychotherapy Training, creator Core Process Psychotherapy. *See* karuna-institute.co.uk

Judith Simmer-Brown, Professor of religious studies Naropa University. *See* naropa.edu

Tami Simon, founder Sounds True Publishing. *See* soundstrue.com

Tai Sutu Rinpoche, Buddhist monk and teacher. *See* kagyu.org

William Spear, author, director Fortunate Blessings Foundation. *See* fortunateblessings.org

Bruce Springsteen, musician and singer. *See* brucespringsteen.net

Tara Stiles, author, founder Strala Yoga and Strala centers worldwide. *See* tarastiles.com

Surya Das Lama, founder Dzogchen Foundation, author *Awakening the Buddha Within. See* surya.org

Robert Thurman, Professor Columbia U, president Tibet House. *See* bobthurman.com

Rama Vernon, activist, yoga teacher. *See* www.americanyogacollege.org

Wavy Gravy, 1960s icon, activist, co-founder Camp Winnarainbow. *See* wavygravy.net

Kirsten Westby, author, human rights activist. *See* kiriwestby.com

Marianne Williamson, motivational speaker, author *A Return to Love.* *See* marianne.com

Made in the USA
Lexington, KY
30 March 2017